for men only

the

secrets

to

pleasuring

a

woman

for men
only

Sharon Colona

Frederick Fell Publishers, Inc.
Hollywood, FLA

Published by
Frederick Fell Publishers, Inc.
2131 Hollywood Boulevard
Hollywood, Florida 33020
800-771-3355
e-mail: fellpub@aol.com

This publication is designed to provide accurate and authoritative information in regard to the subject matter covered. It is sold with the understanding that the publisher is not engaged in rendering legal, accounting, or other professional service. If legal advice or other assistance is required, the services of a competent professional person should be sought. *From A Declaration of Principles jointly adopted by a Committee of the American Bar Association and a Committee of Publishers.*

Printed in Canada
Interior Design by Vicki Heil

Visit our web site at www.fellpub.com

Library of Congress Cataloging-in-Publication Data
Colona, Sharon, 1967—
      For men only : the secrets to pleasuring a woman / by Sharon Colona
         p.   cm.
      ISBN 0-88391-020-9
      1. Sex instruction for men. 2. Sexual excitement. 3. Women-Sexual behavior.
      I. Title.
      Library of Congress Control Number: 00-132831

acknowledgements

I believe that God chooses special people to bring into your life for you to love & learn from; these people help create who you are and who you will become...

With special thanks to the men in my life: Sam, my first love and close friend; John, the most loving man I've known; Terri, the most sincere and innocent; Todd, my constant in a changing world; Derek, who taught me to enjoy life; Pat, who gave me insight and an appreciation of family; and Jeff, who taught me it is not as important to love as it is to show your love. You have all made up different parts of my life and different parts of me. Each of you carry special memories and will always carry a piece of my heart.

To my closest friends, whose support, friendship and encouragement have helped me through all aspects of my life: Donna Maddox, Bob Blumb, Moe Thompson, Lisa Till, Renee Beard, Evvonne Lloyd, Dale Oestriech, Jim Lapides, Roxanne Buss, Dianna Bick, Margie Ellisor, Mark Pollman, Noreen Goldstein, Christine Colona, Joy Pakula, Georgia Brown, Popi Pappas, Sheila Petty, Kristi Redell and Theresa Ruckenbrod.

To my clients and friends who shared their most intimate thoughts and ideas: Your honesty, sincerity and openness made this possible. I could not have written this without you.

To my sister, Autumn: In the yin yang of things, I still wonder what I ever did to be blessed with you in my life. You will always be my truest love.

And finally, to my grandmother: my teacher, my friend, my counselor, my mentor. You are so greatly missed.

table of contents

dedication

This book is dedicated to Daniel G.
Sorry it took so long for an answer.

introduction

*"The great question
that has never been answered and
which I have not yet been able to
answer despite my thirty years of
research into the feminine soul is:
what does a woman want?"*
—Sigmund Freud

Have you ever wanted to get inside a woman's head and just browse around a little to find out what she really thinks, what makes her tick, what pleasures her, her sexual likes and dislikes, etc.? Well, this is your chance. *For Men Only* is an honest, straightforward look into the female mind and anatomy.

The idea for this book first came up about seven years ago. I was out with some friends when a young man who was standing with our group began discussing his new fiancé. After a few hours and a few drinks had gone by, he decided to get candid about his relationship with her. He told me that she was not enjoying sex (achieving an orgasm) and asked what I thought was wrong.

Seeing the surprised look on my face, he decided to add, "I don't have any sisters to talk to about this, no close female friends, and this is something I don't feel comfortable asking my mom about." He was hoping for a quick solution to a big problem. The sincere look on his face made me try to at least grope for some answers. After awkwardly trying to help, I ended up telling him he ought to buy a book on the subject. Although I had the prerequisite of being a female, I had never had any real satisfying sexual relations. In other words, I was definitely not the one to ask.

The next time I was at a bookstore I thought of him and decided to find a book to meet his needs. I found out that although there are a multitude of books on how to satisfy a man in bed, there is little to nothing written on what satisfies a woman. And, surprisingly enough, the few books that I did find were written by men. My first instinct was, "How is a man supposed to know what a woman feels inside or wants sexually?" After reading them, my instinct proved true. Although I had very limited sexual knowledge, I did know the basics of female pleasure and I found some of the information given in these books was not only wrong but sometimes so off the mark it was humorous.

That's when I decided to become an authority and write a book myself. After all, it would be an interesting study and the side effect of improving my own sex life couldn't hurt. At that point, I started to read every book, magazine article, survey and report on a woman's sexuality. As my studies progressed I learned that not only did my friend's fiancé and I have sexual problems, but so did a large majority of the female population.

Having owned and operated a beauty salon for the past eight years, I have had the opportunity to come into constant contact with women of all ages. Once I mentioned I was writing a book on a woman's sexuality, boy did I get some input! Women jumped on the sex bandwagon and gave me every suggestion and complaint they could. Through talking with them I have found that, unfortunately, many women have dissatisfying sexual relationships. Even more unfortunate, most of them never communicate their dissatisfaction.

I have combined my personal experiences, those of my clients, friends and relatives, to come up with information that will prove to be extremely valuable to you. Some of the more informative books I've researched include: *The Cosmo Report, The Janus*

Report and *The Kinsey Report.* All of these are sexual study books with collective statistics of over 150,000 women. In reading this material I have been able to conclude that, although women are of different races, professions and ages, their basic sexual desires are the same.

Even if you have been in a long-term honest relationship and feel you know your partner's sexual needs, I am confident you will find much of this information not only enlightening but sometimes surprising. Women can be extremely inhibited about expressing their sexual desires openly. I am sure that no matter how long you have been with your partner, there is still much you can learn about her sexually.

This is where the following lessons come in. This is your opportunity to discover your partner's needs without her having to talk. I will do all the explaining and hopefully you will do all of the listening. As I've said, the following lessons are not just based on what I believe, but are in agreement with what average, everyday beauty customers have said as well as various professionally recorded reports. It describes what over 150,000 women asked for when surveyed. The following pages are made up of their input. This is their voice. Any one of these women could very easily be your wife or your girlfriend. Please listen with an open mind.

Let the lessons sink in! Read and reread! You might be tempted to skip chapters that you feel you have already mastered, or that you think are not important to your sex life. PLEASE DO NOT SKIP CHAPTERS. Each chapter contains information that will affect a woman's sexuality and pleasure. The chapters that you think are the most ridiculous or the least important are the ones you need to read twice. It makes sense that if you don't think it's important, you are probably not utilizing that skill and your partner is missing the chance to have a completely fulfilling sex life.

Consider this analogy: In an orchestra there are many sections, all of which have well-learned musicians and finely tuned instruments. When brought together they can make a harmonious symphony that is wonderfully pleasing. However, if just one instrument is off key or one musician is poorly prepared, the whole effect can be ruined. Although all of the other musicians sound perfect, a single musician who is off key can stand out, and worse yet, can sabotage the musical performance.

This is an important analogy to remember. Although you might be someone who has 90% of your performance perfect, the 10% that still needs work could be what makes the difference between your receiving a standing ovation or no applause at all. Many times you will find that the little percentage missing is what prohibits a woman from reaching an orgasm. I am excited to be able to provide you with lessons that will collectively teach you to make beautiful music!

Although I believe that the most beautiful orgasmic sex is when you are in a monogamous relationship and sharing yourself with someone that you love, I understand that everyone does not fall into this category. This is why it would be irresponsible of me to write a book about sex and not bring up the issue of safe sex. If you are with a partner who you are not sure is one hundred percent free of sexually transmitted diseases, then always, let me repeat this, ALWAYS, use safe sexual practices.

Throughout this book I do not go into details on how and when to use prophylactics. This is not because of lack of importance. In all honesty, I have always preferred a monogamous relationship with a partner who has supplied to me a clean bill of health. For this reason I am not an expert on using prophylactics. If you have any questions regarding them you should seek counseling from your physician. They will be able to provide you with information and the choices you need to know. Don't worry about prophylactics hindering a woman from achieving orgasm, because I can safely say that no woman will care if you have given her an orgasm if you have also given her a sexually transmitted disease.

I also hope it's safe to say that everyone reading this book knows where babies come from. One repercussion of having great sex is that you will want more of it and so will your partner. With increased sex drive comes an increased chance for reproduction. If having babies is not your goal, always use some form of birth control. And, for anyone out there who believes withdrawal is an effective method of birth control, it is not. It is, at best, a less effective way of getting pregnant. Use an against-all-odds method such as condoms, birth control pills, Noraplant, etc. There are dozens of reliable products available. Again, consult your physician for the method that would best suit your needs.

Studying the sexual woman has been a truly enlightening experience. I believe I have learned more about a woman's sexuality in the last few years than most people learn in a lifetime. It has helped me to better understand my own sexuality. It has also made a big improvement in my own sexual satisfaction — OK — an enormous improvement. An important lesson I have learned is that a woman's ability to achieve orgasm during intercourse can be taught. All you need is a knowledgeable, not necessarily experienced, partner.

By reading this book you will be taking your first step towards an exciting new venture into understanding a woman's wants, needs, fears and inner thoughts. And, although you might find it a bit complex, it will be well worth the study. You will learn to enrich and improve your sex life and create a passion that neither you nor your partner have experienced!

lesson

1

*". . . women that delight in courting
are willing to yield."*
—John Lyly

Enjoyable sex for a woman can be a very complex process. There needs to be an understanding of how the whole process works and when it should actually begin. One of the first lessons you should learn is that a satisfactory sex life does not begin in the bedroom; it begins long before. This is one of the biggest sexual differences between men and women, and the least understood.

If you think about it, the actual sex act can only be done one way (in & out) and then people modify different positions from that basic step. Lots of men tend to believe that knowledge of

I

these different positions will create a pleasant experience for their partner. Not true.

Sex is much more of a mental attitude for women. The up and down motion of sex can be accomplished by just about anyone. It is the prerequisites needed before the actual sex act and foreplay that make a difference; the ability to build sexual excitement and desire are what make up a satisfying sexual partner. That's why this chapter will cover the events that should take place before foreplay.

Since there are so many differences in the sexual mentality between men and women, there might be times when you read a section and think, "What does this have to do with a woman's orgasm?" The answer is: everything! Everything that is mentioned in this chapter has a direct influence on your partner's sexual satisfaction. You might not understand it initially, but trust me on this one, it's important.

For those of you who might read this chapter and think that you are past the dating part of a relationship, let me explain something to you; you should never be past the dating part of a relationship. If you have been married 50 years, a great sex life still begins with dating and it's never too late to start. This is about courtship. No matter who you are or how long you have been in a relationship, this is important, so read and absorb.

● ● ●

DATING ETIQUETTE

> *"It is not enough to conquer: One must*
> *know how to seduce."*
> —Voltaire

I initially thought of calling this section "Everything Your Parents Should Have Taught You," because, for the most part, that is exactly what it is. Throughout my dating years I have found that each man has his own form of dating etiquette. I have a strong belief the differences depend a great deal on his upbringing.

There are certain men I have dated who instinctively know and react with the common courtesies a woman should receive. (Those are what I call the good dates.) And then there are the others who I believe, unfortunately, have just never been taught how to show respect to their partners.

I honestly believe that if all men knew how important the following three steps are in building desire in a woman, there would not be a man alive who wouldn't utilize them. These steps can communicate non-verbal statements which say to a woman, "You are important to me," "I respect you," and "You are worth an extra few minutes of my time."

In learning these techniques you are, in essence, learning to stimulate a woman's emotions. You will make her feel important and good about herself, and in turn will aid in her attraction to you and her sexual enjoyment. For a woman, you need not only be visually attractive, but also emotionally and mentally attractive.

Dating etiquette is a very simple lesson to learn. There are only three steps to remember, and for the little effort that is needed, the results can be tremendous. I believe a woman should be shown respect at all times and am confident that after reading how simple these steps are, you will become the gentleman every woman desires. And, if you believe you already know these basic steps, a refresher course never hurts. Remember, while reading, be sure to ask yourself when the last time you utilized them was and, if it has been a while, why?

 **Step 1 — Doors**

I purposely put this first because this one is a given. Always open the door for a woman. Most men seem to know this basic rule at some time, but somewhere along the line either forget or don't want to be bothered, or maybe think that there is some imaginary time line when it isn't necessary anymore. It is always important; it symbolizes respect and, no matter how long you have been with someone, it's an easy and effective way to show consideration.

Car doors — I am constantly surprised at the different variations of the car door opening and closing step. The first variation is when you just get in on your side, reach over and pull up the lock up for the girl — please — way tacky. Then there's the variation where you unlock her door from the outside without opening it, then leave to get in on your side — just as bad. And sometimes, just when you almost have it down, you unlock the door, open it up, invite her to get in, and then walk away without shutting the door.

4

Opening a woman's car door is not only a symbol of respect, but is also a safety precaution. A woman can be extremely vulnerable to purse snatching or an attack, while standing in a parking lot waiting for you to get in and unlock her car door.

There is only one proper way: Unlock her side first, let her in, close the door, get in on your side. Simple.

Upright doors — This one you have to prepare for and think about ahead in order to pull it off with finesse. When approaching any door, take a good three to four steps ahead so you reach the door first, and pull it open. Sounds simple, huh? Yet, I have seen people who have actually pulled the door open and hit their partner. I have even seen women stand and wait for the door to be opened while the guy is standing and waiting for her to open it. Because of the numerous times I have witnessed poor door opening habits and, unfortunately, have been involved in some, I can honestly tell you that doing it the right way makes a difference.

Elevator doors — You can always tell who the true gentleman in the crowd is when waiting for an elevator. He will always be the one who extends his hand for the women to get on first.

Front doors — It is proper and considerate to drop off your partner at the front door to any entrance before parking your car. It is somewhat acceptable to do this only in extreme weather conditions such as rain or snow.

Now, in your mind's eye, you are one of two people reading this. You are either the guy who always does this perfectly out of habit and thinks it's ridiculous for me to even take the time to mention anything about opening doors, or, two, you're the guy whose door opening inadequacies I've just described, who might think it's not important, or it's too picky, or that it is the nineties and women can open their own doors. Whatever you might be thinking right now, know this: It's basic, it's important, it doesn't take any time or a significant amount of effort, and to most women it means a lot.

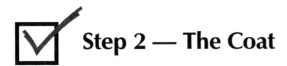 ## Step 2 — The Coat

Pick it up, help her put it on. Again: basic, easy and respectful. To be able to do it with style, remember to always be one step ahead of the game. Women are notoriously late, so while she is getting ready, get her coat out and have it waiting. When leaving a restaurant or theater, pick it up for her, or, if she picks it up first, extend your hand and ask if you can help her with it.

I remember the first man who picked up my coat and helped me put it on. To him it was a basic instinct — something his parents had taught him always to do. To me, I felt like I had just found a prize in my cracker jacks; if he only knew at the time how much respect he gained and how good he made me feel with such a small gesture.

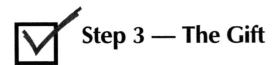 ## Step 3 — The Gift

This is an important one but does not have to be done on every date. A small "thinking of you" gift is always a big brownie point when trying to make a woman feel special and desired. Some of my favorites are: a single flower, a bouquet of flowers, a card that you have placed in the car seat so that she finds it when leaving with you on your date, a bottle of her favorite wine, perfume, chocolates, a poem, a love letter... Really, the list can get as extensive as your imagination. Once again, a small token of affection goes a long way.

● ● ●

I cannot say enough about the importance of these seemingly small gestures of dating etiquette. When my girlfriends and clients confide in me about their dates with different men, this is always the first thing mentioned. Was he a gentleman? In essence: Was he a good date, someone she respected and felt respect from?

One of the most common complaints I hear from married women is that they miss the dating and the common mannerisms that dating people have. They miss that little bit of feeling important and feeling special.

This is where so many mental blocks begin. As you read through I am hoping you will start to see all the different links that stop a woman from letting herself go, from allowing herself to truly enjoy her sexuality. By learning these three basic steps in dating you will help to break down any mental blocks dealing with a woman's self-confidence. Does he respect me? Am I important? Does he desire me? These can sometimes be subliminal mental blocks of which your partner might not even be aware.

Also, the basic dating techniques have a lot to do with the romantic part of a relationship. If you're not familiar with this, repeat after me, "ro-mance."

See, that wasn't too hard. Although many men don't seem to have this word in their vocabulary, romance is one of the most

7

crucial ingredients needed to satisfy a woman's sexual pleasure. Get use to reading about romance because you will find it will come up in almost every chapter.

If you don't believe how much women desperately need romance, take a walk down the fiction isles of a bookstore — one romance novel after the next. It's a multi-billion dollar industry; they thrive on women who are so badly lacking romance in their own lives, that they live vicariously through fictional characters. The writers of these novels understand the importance of romance in dating and ALWAYS have a little of both in their novels before incorporating the actual sex act. They know that without the romance it would just be a sex book that really wouldn't excite a woman. It is the same in a relationship; it is close to impossible to excite a woman without romance.

● ● ●

SEXUAL GROOMING

"I cannot get excited about being with a man that has poor grooming habits."
—Donna Maddox

Here is another topic that you either know and live by faithfully or you don't. There is not a lot of gray area here. Sexual grooming is important because, just as a man is attracted to a female who looks, feels, and smells good, a woman is attracted to a man. These are basics, but once again, we are going to cover them because, believe me, there are those out there who don't have this area quite down pat.

Cologne — Do not overdo the cologne or aftershave. Cologne should be put on so that a woman has to draw closer to you to smell it. If it is overpowering or overbearing it will make her want to get away from you. It seems pretty simple, yet I have been stuck on crowded elevators, at 7:00 a.m., with such bad cologne wars (you know, my cologne is stronger than your cologne) going on that I wished automatic oxygen masks would fall out of the ceiling to help. The common rule of thumb should be: go lightly. Do not go for that extra little splash and, if you are still not sure, ask someone you trust if they think the cologne is too strong.

Eyebrows — Now, this may vary. Different women like different things, but for my own peace of mind, I have to give my input. Eyebrows should be just that — eyebrows — two separate entities. Obviously, many of you are not going to wander into a beauty salon for an eyebrow arch or get out the tweezers every morning and pluck them out one by one, but running a razor down the middle is a good idea. And, the tweezer thing probably isn't a bad idea for those long stray hairs that tend to stick out.

Nose Hairs — Let me put it to you this way: Could you have an orgasm with a girl who had nose hairs sticking out? It's a distraction to say the least. Trim them.

Feet — This is an area where many men do not pay attention. Once again, if you do not feel comfortable going into a salon and having a pedicure done (which would be my first choice, and you probably would thoroughly enjoy the pampering), then at least make sure your toenails are trimmed and you do not have any big, hard calluses. This helps diminish unnecessary distractions that can arise. You always want one hundred percent focus on you and your partner sexually. You do not want your partner wishing in the back of her mind that you would stop rubbing your scratchy feet up against her legs because it's hurting, or annoying, or both.

Pubic Hair — I told you this was going to be straightforward and honest didn't I?

This is also a matter of preference for each individual woman, but I would bank on at least ninety five percent of all women agreeing that nicely trimmed pubic hair is much more attractive and clean looking than just letting nature take its course.

Women have to deal with this situation every day for their bikini line. Some women even have their bikini line waxed, which is, if you are not familiar with it, when hot melted wax is poured onto your pubic area, dried, then ripped off so that all the hairs are pulled out at the root. Sounds fun, huh? Although men are lucky enough to only have to trim with either scissors or a beard trimmer, amazingly enough, some still don't. To put it bluntly, this is unattractive. I am sure most of you have not ever seen the insides of a *Playgirl* magazine, but this would be a good time just to take a peek. Because the editors of this magazine know what women like to see, within the pages you will find only nicely trimmed men.

Beyond the fact that it's much more eye appealing, it is also more hygienic, and when it comes to oral sex, it makes it much more enjoyable for the female. And, the final bonus to neat trimming: By deleting even one inch of hair you have just increased your penis length visibly an inch. How can you go wrong?

Breath — Bad breath can kill a mood in a heartbeat. How can a woman (or anyone, for that matter) concentrate on enjoying the moment when she is kissing someone with bad breath? Gum and breath fresheners are your friends; use them. If you smoke and your partner doesn't, try to make a concentrated effort to keep your breath fresh at all times, there's nothing quite like kissing an ashtray.

● ● ●

DR. JECKLE/MR. HYDE

"What have you done for me lately?"
—Janet Jackson

As you read through the *Dating Etiquette* section, I am confident there were areas that rang familiar — techniques you have possibly used before. If so, now is the time to update your habits further.

A personal pet peeve of mine, and one that I am confident is shared by many other women, is the "Dr. Jeckle/Mr. Hyde" syndrome. Often men start a relationship on their best behavior; they bring you flowers, open your car door, shower you with compliments, etc. Then, as the relationship progresses, the politeness diminishes. And I know it's not only men, many women fall into a "Ms. Jeckle/Ms. Hyde" category.

If your partner falls into this category, I am sure you are thinking: "What happened to my five course dinner, her hair and make-up, her sex drive, and why is everything so different?" On the other hand, women are thinking: "What happened to my romantic dinners out, those passionate kisses, all of the compliments and did he forget how to open the passenger car door?"

A lot of people argue that it's a comfort level you reach after you have been in a relationship for a while. It doesn't sound very comfortable to me, and since I have been there before, I can tell you it doesn't feel too comfortable, either. For a woman, it feels like you don't care about her and you don't think her important enough to do those little things. Obviously, these are not the type of feelings that will increase your partner's sex drive.

In order to successfully improve your sex life, you must first analyze the way you treat your partner in a relationship. Do you treat her with respect? Do you treat her as you did when you first met? If not, why has it changed? Many people complain about their sex life deteriorating during their relationship. But, I've found the truth behind the complaint is that their relationship is deteriorating and as a result, their sex life suffers.

One of the most disappointing things I have ever heard was on a morning talk show. The show was discussing the signs to look for if your man is having an affair. The top signs were: taking a new interest in his looks; a new hair style; more exercise; credit card receipts from florists, hotels and lingerie stores; and buying his own new underwear.

This is not only disappointing but also frustrating. I believe sometimes men look for excitement and newness in a relationship, and they think they can only get that with someone other than their partner. They do not consider introducing a new excitement into their current relationship. Why not take your current partner to a hotel? Or send her flowers for no reason? Or buy her sexy lingerie? It seems to me that too many people start looking for something that they already have; somewhere along the line they just forget they already have it.

Although it is understandable that no one can be on their best behavior all of the time, there doesn't seem to be a happy medium. Many times the first month in a relationship is the best treatment you are ever going to get. By the end of the year you are with a totally new person. A close friend of mine was talking about her husband and said, "The only thing my husband has in common with the man I married is that they look the same." This holds true for too many people. I understand people change throughout their lifetime, but the basic respect and treatment of your partner should not.

If you and your partner are stuck in a "comfortable" relationship, take initiative! I am sure you remember how you treated your partner when you first started dating, and since you have just read the basics on dating, you should use them. Do not get stuck in a catch-22 situation where you don't want to put in the effort until she does. Somebody has to be the first one to start for change to occur. With every step taken you will be closer to a completely satisfying sexual relationship for you and your partner.

● ● ●

THE PERFECT KISS

> *"I don't remember the first kiss, I remember the first good kiss."*
> —Angie Dickenson

There is not enough that can be said about kissing; kissing, if done right, is one of the most sensual experiences two people can have. Unfortunately, since there have never been classes available on kissing, men have had to learn on their own.

13

Although most hope that they are doing a good job of it, there are some who need a little improvement.

I was having a conversation with a friend of mine who has been married about four years. She hates the way her husband kisses her. When I asked her why she wouldn't tell him, or have him sit still while she kissed him the way she liked, she said that it made her feel uncomfortable. "After all these years how am I suppose to tell my husband that I don't like the way he kisses me?" She was worried she might hurt his feelings and make him self-conscious when he kissed her, or worse yet, make him so mad he didn't want to kiss her again. Because none of these are conducive to a good sexual relationship, I am going to explain how to give the perfect kiss, the kind of kiss every woman wants — passionate, sensual and romantic.

Have you ever noticed how couples kiss in really romantic movies? It's not just a kiss; it's an experience in itself. They gaze into each other's eyes and whisper sweet nothings. He holds her face gently in his hands and then slowly goes in for the kiss. The experience is at least five minutes in itself. Now that is what I am talking about; not just a kiss — the kiss.

Let's start with the gaze, the foreplay to the kiss. Work yourself within inches of her face (not too close or you will look cross-eyed) and gaze into her eyes for just a moment. Look around her face and notice her lips, the curves of her cheeks, her whole face. It makes it a lot more appealing if you are thinking about how beautiful she is. I don't know why, but women can instinctively tell from your eye contact if you like what you see. A gentle touch of your fingers down her cheek can also be a nice touch.

If you really feel like you're getting the hang of it, this is the time to whisper wonderful things she likes to hear: "You are so

14

beautiful," "I love you so much," "You are so sexy," "You're gorgeous," "You have the most beautiful eyes I've ever seen," "You're incredible," "I love you." Any of these statements will work perfectly. Now, gently — very gently — hold her face with one or both hands and slowly go for the kiss. The first kiss should be a light touch to the lips, almost a brush. Then, pull back in a teasing way, slowly working your way into a more passionate kiss. A passionate kiss is not defined by pushing and prodding your tongue in her mouth. A passionate kiss happens when you are probing and exploring not just her mouth, but her neck, ears, etc. The key word here is gentle; always be gentle when kissing. Being gentle does not mean you shouldn't be passionate, especially in the heat of the moment, just don't be overbearing. Know your limits.

An additional way to be very sensual when kissing is to lick your lips. I once saw a movie with Christian Slater, where he did the face hold move, while whispering sweet nothings to the girl. Then, before he kissed her, he licked his lips as if in anticipation to what he knew was coming — THAT WAS HOT! I, in addition to many other women, re-wound the movie, played it back and re-wound it again. It was enough to give me goose bumps.

Don't forget a woman not only has lips, but also shoulders, a neck and ears. Don't be afraid to peruse around a bit. Even a soft kiss to the forehead can be wonderfully exciting if done tenderly and romantically.

The most important points to remember are: *gently, softly,* and *tenderly*. In other words — *romantically*. Once you have mastered this kiss, you will be able to make a woman melt. By just adding a few special touches, you can turn an average kiss into a wonderful, sensual experience.

15

The main reason I am so detailed in describing the perfect kiss is throughout life, whenever a girlfriend of mine would get one of these kisses, I would have to listen to a play by play account of the kiss. "Then he said this, then he did that" and "Ooh was he the greatest kisser." Because I have been fortunate enough to have been on the receiving end of a few, I can honestly say that if done right, it can take your breath away.

Compatibility when kissing is important to a quality relationship and sex life. As I have mentioned, I have been on the receiving end of some great kisses, but I have also had kisses that were not just bad, but downright horrible. There is nothing worse than trying to be romantic with someone who you don't enjoy kissing.

Here are some basic no no's when kissing:

- **Slobbering**—there is no need to secrete a lot of excess fluids in someone's mouth. A kiss should be moist, not wet.

- **Face Swallowing**—Do not try to consume your partner's face when kissing. Your kissing practices should not resemble eating an ice cream cone.

- **Tongue Jamming**—This is not the time to see how far your tongue can reach down your partner's throat. When in doubt, gentle is better.

- **Repetitiveness**—If you have ever kissed a person who darts their tongue in and out of your mouth in the exact same way for the entire kissing episode, it can make you feel like you are kissing a computer. Gently probe and explore.

■ **Overbearing**—Some men do not know their own strength. When kissing, they overpower you with their tongue and lips. Women are typically more fragile than men and what you might not feel is rough, can be completely overwhelming for them.

These are just some ways to add to your kissing style. The best way to tell if your partner is enjoying how you kiss her is to ask her to show you how she would like to be kissed. Tell her you want to see how she would give her most seducing, romantic kiss, then sit back, take notes and enjoy.

There is nothing wrong with communicating your preferences in a relationship, especially with something so simple as kissing. Maybe you don't like the way she kisses you. Show her how you would like to be kissed and then work on a compromise that is mutually satisfying for both of you.

● ● ●

ANSWERS TO COMMON QUESTIONS

"If I were asked for a one line answer to the question, 'What makes a woman good in bed?' I would say, a man who is good in bed."
—Bob Guccione

 W hile writing this book, I not only interviewed women for their opinions, but also men. I wanted to cover the things important to a woman and also to answer any questions men might have.

 It turned out there were more questions than I had bargained for, actually enough for an entire book in itself. I have narrowed the questions down to the most asked questions dealing specifically with a woman's sexuality.

 Even though we are in the nineties, unfortunately, a lot of people are still uncomfortable talking about sex. It can be an intimidating subject, especially to men. Many men believe that they are instinctively supposed to know everything about sex and asking questions would be admitting that they don't. So, in turn, they don't ask.

Another problem is: Who do you ask if you are not in a relationship or have a close friend who is a female? Asking if your penis size is important in satisfying a woman is typically not a question you ask your mother. And, by asking another male you would once again be admitting your sexual knowledge deficiency. Besides, more than likely, any man you ask is probably seeking answers to the same questions himself.

The following are the most frequently asked questions, with unbiased, honest answers.

●　●　●

HOW CAN I TELL IF MY PARTNER IS SEXUALLY SATISFIED?

"He always has an orgasm and doesn't wait for me. It's unfair."
—Lorena Bobbit

Ask her. Although it sounds simple enough, almost too simple, it is amazing how many people never talk about sex and never ask questions. When different men have asked me this question, I ask them if they think their partner is satisfied. Usually the answer is "yes". And when I ask them how they know, the answers range from, "Because she has never complained" to "I can just tell."

I have yet to come across someone who said they know their partner is satisfied because he talks to her about sex, because he has had detailed conversations with her about her desires and

20

fantasies, and what she does and doesn't like. For some strange reason, this is an awkward subject to talk about. I find it ironic that two people close enough to have intercourse do not feel close enough to talk it over.

Even if you are confident that your partner is satisfied and you feel that you are the greatest lover in the world, I believe there is always room for improvement on both sides. The only real way to know if your partner is truly happy with your current sexual relationship is to open up the lines of communication. I don't just mean for you to ask her if she's satisfied, and when she answers "yes," that's the end of it. Find out what she likes in particular, create a conversation based around it, and let her know how important it is to you. Ask if there is anything in particular she doesn't like, or something she might like to try.

The next few chapters are going to give you information on the basics of understanding a woman's sexuality and her sexual needs to achieve an orgasm. What I can't tell you, though, is personal information such as what position she likes the most, does she like hand manipulation better left to right, up and down or in circles — all the detailed information you are going to have to acquire from her through communication.

You will NEVER really know if you are satisfying your partner until you talk about her sexual preferences. Hearing her moan and groan and maybe even scream does not tell you if she is satisfied. Many women have writhed around, moaned and groaned and not had a minute's worth of satisfaction. The extreme pleasure you may believe your partner is having very well may be little more than good showmanship (which we will cover in lesson three).

When you communicate, not only have you given yourself a great opportunity to find out what your partner wants, but also an opportunity to let her know what you want. A lot of women don't believe their sexual satisfaction is important, and just by letting her know that it is, is a big step that I'm sure she will appreciate.

IS SIZE IMPORTANT?

"What matters is not the length of the wand,
but the magic in the stick."
—Anonymous

Size is not important. *The Kinsey Institute New Report on Sex* states: "The vast majority of men measure within the average genital size range and have a penis that is approximately five to seven inches long when erect, a length that is more than adequate for sexual functioning. Actual difficulties with sexual function or reproduction, rarely occur unless the erect penis is less than two inches long." In other words, unless you are less than two inches long while fully erect, you have nothing to worry about. As a matter of fact, I have often heard complaints from women who experience pain during intercourse because their partners are too big.

A woman's genitalia is made with the nerve endings (the sensors), mainly on the outside of the vagina. The clitoris, located on the outside, is the most sensitive area for stimulation or an orgasm. During intercourse, the groin area above the penis rubs against a woman's clitoris and stimulates her to an orgasm. Your penis size is not important for this stimulation.

I tend to believe that the only part penis size plays in a woman's sexual pleasure is psychological. For a woman to allow a man to enter her, to actually be inside of her body, is a mental stimulation. It is a sharing of herself, a bond and a closeness.

Since you are now coming to realize that women's orgasms are more mentally based than physical, you should see that even though penetration is important for mental stimulation, the size of the penetrator is not.

If you are still concerned with the length of your penis interfering in your sex life, there are many sexual positions that can deepen your penetration. Any type of rear entry (when you are behind your partner) such as doggy style or having your partner bend over across a chair or bed while you enter her from behind, provides deep penetration. A word of caution, this can often be painful for your partner if you are above average in penis size. Go slow and see what makes her comfortable.

If you are a man who has been insecure with the size of his penis, now is the time to let go of those insecurities. Women know that a small penis does not interfere with sexual fulfillment and, if anything, can make intercourse a more pleasurable and less painful experience. I just wish all of those macho men who talk about their twelve inches could figure this out.

HOW CAN I TELL IF A WOMAN HAS HAD AN ORGASM?

"The only time a woman has a true orgasm is when she is shopping. Every other time she is faking it. It's common courtesy."
—Joan Rivers

You can't.

I don't want to put it so point-blank, but many men I have talked to seem to think they can and they can't. You can't. Nobody can. I just want to clear the record. Have you ever

23

watched the scene in *When Harry Met Sally,* when Meg Ryan and Billy Chrystal are sitting in the restaurant and she shows him how to fake an orgasm? What many men don't realize is, not only is that a funny scene, it is a true scene.

Contrary to popular belief, there is no proverbial light switch that goes on when a woman has an orgasm. I have heard that when a woman has an orgasm, she secretes more fluid, and that's how you can tell. The truth is, a woman secretes fluid when she is excited — a lot of fluid. And when she has an orgasm, there is not a distinguishable amount more. I have heard, "You can just tell, if you know what you're doing." Again, wrong. I hate to burst any bubbles, but I don't care how good in bed you are, you cannot tell if a woman has orgasmed.

The Kinsey Institute New Report On Sex states: "There is no way to be certain if orgasm has actually occurred short of having the woman wired to a huge array of physiological measurement instruments to monitor blood pressure, heart rate, vaginal contractions, brain activity and all other indicators of arousal and orgasm. Of course, you'd also need experts on hand to interpret the readings." These are doctors who study sexuality as a profession; I think they are pretty credible.

This seems to be a pride thing with a lot of men. They not only believe they can tell if their partner has orgasmed — they know they can — no two ways about it. It's as if they feel they would be an inadequate lover without this knowledge or, by admitting they can't tell, would also be admitting women may have faked with them in the past.

My first sexual boyfriend and I dated for three years. I am confident he thought we had the best sex ever. We tried every position known to man. We had sex five to seven nights a week and I faked orgasms five to seven nights a week. If he ever reads this, he won't believe it, but when you are faking five to seven nights a week, you get it down to a fine science. It is nothing for the two of us to be ashamed about, at the time neither one of us were sexually experienced and we both had a lot of learning to do. Actually, I consider myself lucky; I know many women who are married who have NEVER had an orgasm in their life and their husbands would die if they knew.

The closest you will ever come to being able to tell if your partner has had an orgasm is by having a partner who communicates with you openly and honestly. Other than that, you can give it your all and hope for the best; only she will know for sure.

WHAT DO WOMEN WANT FROM MEN?

"Woman is man's confusion."
—Vincent of Beauvais

One of the biggest differences between men and women is that women have orgasms with their mind and men have orgasms with their penis. Don't get me wrong, there is physical stimulation needed for a woman to achieve ultimate sexual pleasure, but her main sexuality stems from the heart and, if you really want to get deep, from her soul.

Women equate sex with love, caring, tenderness, and respect, and consider it to be a bond between two people. Men tend to have a more physical approach. One example of the two differences is with masturbation. When women masturbate, they create mental fantasies that are very detailed and elaborate and then work their way into an orgasm through

25

their fantasy. I have known men to take a shower and within ten minutes, not only had time to wash their body and shampoo their hair, but fit in an orgasm to boot.

It may sound corny, but what a woman truly wants is your understanding of the differences you both have and your consideration. By consideration, I do not only mean your understanding that a woman's sexuality stems from her mind; but that you must act upon this and be willing to modify your lovemaking skills. Her needs should be an important aspect of your sexual relationship. Learn about her desires and then put in the time and patience to modify your sexual practices to meet her needs. And, while discovering what is important to her, you will have the opportunity to learn about your own sexual desires.

Let me give you an analogy: Anyone can play golf. They can swing a club, walk the course, drive the cart, and use all of the same clubs a professional uses. But, until they really know the game, until they are willing to take time and effort to practice different techniques, they will never be the potentially great golfer they could be. (I purposely used the golf analogy in case there are any men reading this who are wondering, "Is this time and effort to satisfy my partner really worth it?", because I'm just wondering how many hours have been spent practicing golf.)

I hope that you not only read this book but also absorb the information given. After all, it is up to you to show your partner she is well worth the time and effort it takes to understand a woman's sexual differences.

IS THERE A DIFFERENCE BETWEEN A MALE AND FEMALE ORGASM?

"All orgasms are magical in their own right."
—*Sex Secrets*

One of the most detailed researches done on the male and female orgasm makes up Master's and Johnson's *Human Sexual Response.* The study compares the physical changes that occur during the male and female orgasm. Their research has shown many similarities including an increase in blood pressure, sex flush and muscle spasms. This information would tend to make you believe the male and female orgasm feels the same. However, since there are no ways of gauging how each individual feels, there can be no conclusive answer.

Although men and women describe the same physical pleasures when achieving an orgasm, the reasons for reaching an orgasm can be extremely different. Men have the ability to consistently reach an orgasm through a variety of different situations. For example: A man can be highly aroused and achieve orgasm by an extremely sexual female even though he has no emotional or physical attachment; a woman in the same situation is much less likely to have an orgasm.

Men tend to need only one attraction to achieve orgasm while women are more complex, requiring multiple stimuli. A woman's orgasm is based on many factors. Is she physically attracted to her mate? Does she feel an emotional attachment? Is she sexually aroused by him? Is he mentally stimulating to her? All of these issues combined are what gives a woman the ability to have an orgasm on a consistent basis with her partner.

Although the combination of stimuli is necessary, I believe the emotional attachment has the largest influence on a woman's orgasm. Does she trust you? Does she care about (love) you? Does she feel respect from you? This is why I have placed so much emphasis on the prerequisites of sex. Contrary to a man's orgasm, the actual sex act in itself has minimal effect on a woman's orgasm.

This is extremely important to remember when trying to understand a woman's sexuality and what is needed in order for her to achieve an orgasm on a regular basis. You must understand that, although you might be able to achieve an orgasm with minimal effort, your partner requires a multitude of stimuli to reach that same plateau.

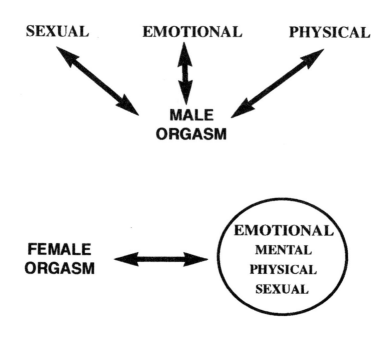

28

The diagram illustrates the differences between men and women in the achievement of an orgasm.

All of the complexities involved in a woman achieving an orgasm can seem overwhelming. I'm sure it is especially hard to comprehend if your own satisfaction requires minimal effort. Although exploring the differences between the male and female sexuality require many trial and error experiments, I am confident that you will find this type of learning can be extremely fun; I wouldn't be surprised if you learn more about your own sexual pleasures in the process.

WHAT IS THE MOST COMMON COMPLAINT WOMEN HAVE ABOUT SEX?

"If a woman's emotional needs are not met, she can't respond to you physically."
—Ellen Kreidman

Simple answer: Romance. Remember that word we learned earlier?

This might not be the answer you want to hear. It is not hot and exciting, and it probably is the last complaint a man would have about sex. If you are like most men, romance plays a very small part in your sexual satisfaction. However, the lack of romance is the number one complaint among women. Remember, a woman's most important sexual organ is her mind.

Let's talk a little about how these sexual differences started in the first place. Why is romance so important to a woman? If you think about it, romance is introduced to girls at a very young age. Snow White, Sleeping Beauty and Cinderella were our first romance novels. While boys were out playing with trucks and guns, girls were reading about Prince Charming, who was handsome, kind, gentle, loving. I'm sure he was a figment of someone's imagination, yet he was exactly what all little girls wanted: A romantic, handsome man who had a horse, a big castle and who would do anything in the world for his princess.

Okay, so you don't have a horse or a castle, but you can still be a prince. You just need to add a little romance into your relationship. In order to sexually arouse a woman, she needs to be attracted to you, not just physically attracted, more importantly, she needs to be attracted to who you are and how you make her feel outside of the bedroom.

Please don't think that you have to change your entire personality, but even a small change for the better in the romance department will work wonders. If you are completely lost and have never been romantic, try some of these ideas: A surprise homemade candlelight dinner for two; flowers for no reason, just because; a night where you turn off your favorite sporting event, just to sit outside under the stars and talk; a surprise horse and carriage ride; a surprise picnic lunch. When was the last time you've taken her dancing? If you're on a tight budget, light some candles, turn on the radio and use the living room as your dance floor.

These suggestions seem basic and simple to me (being a woman), but they hardly ever happen. Or, when they do, often it is within the first few months of dating, never to be seen again afterwards.

Think about it for a minute. When was the last time you were romantic? Have you ever been? And, if not, why? I imagine if you are concerned about your partner's sexual satisfaction, you care for her. Why not occasionally show her?

Just because romance might not be a large part of your sexual desire, do not think for one minute this holds true for your partner. Just as you would like her to greet you at the door in nothing but a garter belt, so would she like to cuddle and hear sweet nothings in her ear. Get the picture? If you are trying to enhance your sex life, for a moment, set aside what you think would be enjoyable and think about what a woman would find enjoyable.

For most women, their best sexual experiences have been with a romantic, caring, nurturing partner. This is no coincidence. For women, sex and romance go hand in hand. It is hard to explain, but a woman must feel respected, important and cared for before she can be completely uninhibited in the bedroom. She has to desire the person she is with, and it is up to you to be desirable.

If I were going to give a homework assignment to every man, I would start by asking them to read *Romance 101* and *1001 Ways to be Romantic,* both by Gregory J.P. Godek. These are helpful books in learning about the mental connection to women. They define romance, and being the newly reformed romantic that you are, I'm confident you will want to expand your horizons in as many ways as you can.

WHY DOES MY PARTNER ALWAYS HAVE A HEADACHE?

"Not now, I have a headache."
—Unknown

Many therapists report the most common reason for a lack of sexual interest is hidden anger or frustration. Everyone holds in their feelings or represses anger at one time or another, but when it starts to interfere with your sexual relations it should be realized as a problem that needs to be dealt with.

Deeply rooted frustration stems from a lack of response. If your partner has expressed a particular dissatisfaction in your relationship and there is lack of response, it can bring resentment. Let me give you an example: If your partner is upset because she feels you flirt with other women and you do not acknowledge her feelings, she will in turn harbor her resentment. Most people have a tendency to pull their anger inward, if showing it outwardly has not acquired results.

This is not to say you should always give in to your partner to have a quality sex life. However, you do need to confront the situation, acknowledge her feelings, and come to an understanding. These three steps can save you and your partner a lot of frustration and anguish.

Many times women have a tendency to keep their frustrations pent up, with the expectation that their partner should assume something is wrong and then choose to discuss it. There are two things wrong with this thought process. One, most men are not extremely intuitive when it comes to women, and two, most men are not masters at communication.

If your partner harbors this type of thought process you can help stop the building up of tension before it starts. Sit her down and let her know that you are not a mind reader, that her feelings are important to you, and that she needs to let you know when something is wrong or else you both cannot work on a solution.

Although pent up frustration is the number one reason men and women "have a headache," there are also many other factors that might be affecting your partner. I am confident that after reading all the lessons you will be able to better recognize the specific problems that might be affecting your relationship and have the knowledge to solve them.

● ● ●

lesson

3

WHY WOMEN
FAKE ORGASMS

"To know how to live is to know how to simulate."
—Antoinette Deshoulieres

W hile acquiring information for this book, I asked many male friends and acquaintances for their opinions on women faking an orgasm. Interesting enough, none of the men who I had spoken with ever knew a woman to fake an orgasm. Not only that, but they assured me that their partners were completely satisfied. I felt very fortunate to have always spoken to men who were completely fulfilling. As a matter of fact, I am confident I spoke to over 50 men about this book and all 50 never had a woman fake an orgasm (and they can tell) and they have always brought a woman to a minimum of one orgasm in every sexual session. Huh...

If you are a numbers type of guy, here are some interesting numbers for you: The *Janus Report* surveyed 1,398 women and 1,341 men, revealing that 65% of the men always had an orgasm during intercourse compared to only 15% of the women. Sixteen percent of the women said they rarely or never have had an orgasm, compared to 4% of the men. To make this clearer, out of every 100 women, 15% are satisfied with their sex life. With these type of statistics, there is a lot of room for improvement.

The good thing to remember is, since women have an emotional attachment to sex, the fact that they do not always orgasm doesn't necessarily mean that they aren't enjoying it. Since I think it may be hard for some men to understand how anyone can enjoy sex without achieving orgasm, I have another analogy for you: Imagine you are going to your favorite sporting event and your favorite team is playing. Your team might not win, but aren't you happy to be there anyway? Don't you have a great time just being at the game with all the excitement? O.K., so it would have been better if your team had won, but all in all you enjoyed it and you would definitely do it again. That experience is the same as a woman having sex without an orgasm.

In the following chapter you will find out why many women find it necessary to fake an orgasm. I believe a lot of men not only dislike the idea of their partner faking an orgasm, but in some ways feel patronized or even deceived. This is a barrier that needs to be broken down.

If a woman is to communicate her sexual dissatisfaction, she needs to know that you are ready to hear and learn from them. If she thinks the repercussions of her honesty are going to make a bad situation worse, she will never tell you her true feelings.

A question you have to ask yourself is: If your partner is faking orgasm, is this something you really want to know? Ask yourself this question before talking with your partner. There are many times it is necessary for open communication in order to improve your sex life. However, if you are not mentally ready for one of these open, honest talks it could cause more damage than good.

Please keep an open mind when reading this chapter. Faking an orgasm has been around as long as sex has. I don't know a woman who hasn't faked an orgasm at least once in her life. I hope that after reading this chapter you will begin to understand it is not a true deception; it falls into the little white lie category that doesn't hurt anyone except the person who tells the little white lie.

● ● ●

A WOMAN'S ROLE IN SOCIETY

> *"Aren't women prudes if they don't*
> *and prostitutes if they do?"*
> —Kate Millet

A misconception that affects some women is that they shouldn't want or enjoy sex. They believe sex is dirty and they are less than proper if they want it. During the course of marriage, sex is a responsibility that they must perform the same as cooking or cleaning. These are old-fashioned ideas, but ideas that are still fixtures in the minds of many women.

A man can be more open with his sexuality without fear of persecution. Men who have a lot of sexual partners can brag about their experiences. Given the same situation, a woman would be put into the "tramp" category. Throughout the years, society has given men and women completely different sexual standards to live by. Women are taught at a young age to be wholesome and pure; they are told that's the kind of girl men want. Yet, on the other hand, there has never been any importance put on giving the same advice to young men.

Don't get me wrong. I am not saying that raising a girl to be wholesome is wrong; I am saying their sexual freedom is by far more limited throughout their life and therefore shows up limited in the bedroom.

After years of sexual repression, most women find it uncomfortable to express what they want and need: If she is not enjoying herself, and she tells you, will she seem like a tramp? If she tells you she wants to experiment, will she feel like a whore, or worse yet, will you think of her as a whore? Is it all right to have sexual fantasies? Is it all right for her to initiate sex? All of this comes into play when dealing with a woman's sexuality. I also believe it has a lot to do with the fact that women don't orgasm as frequently in the bedroom. Women typically are more inhibited and don't feel free to express themselves.

If you were made to feel self conscious about acting sexual, how do you think it would affect your sex life? If a man felt that it was immoral or improper to initiate sex with a woman, imagine the detrimental impact on sexual relations. If men didn't initiate the sex in 80% of relationships, there would be no sex. I am positive that had society reversed the roles, women would not only be as sexual but probably more sexual than men. Some women are stuck in a world where they don't feel they can release all of their inhibitions and sexual desires without repercussion. If your partner is consciously or unconsciously holding back, she will never be able to experience an orgasm.

Now, what can you do about it? You can help change the way a woman thinks about sex. You should encourage her to be as sexual as she wants; ask her about her fantasies, ask her about her desires. Give her the security she needs and the confidence. Let your words and actions define your respect for her. Tell her that it is important to you that she expresses her sexual desires.

Many times, after a woman goes through childbirth, she starts to feel uncomfortable with her sexuality. She might suppress her desires out of fear that they are not appropriate anymore, taking on a role that a good mother does not have unbridled, nasty sex.

Once again, this is a role society has forced on women which can affect your partner's sexual satisfaction, as well as your own. Your partner might be a mom but she is still a sexual woman and should be treated as such. Take her to a hotel, far away from children, and give her encouragement to express her sexuality. Having children may alter your sexual practices but they should not diminish them.

● ● ●

SELF ESTEEM

"Never are you more naked than when you are naked in front of a man."
—Nancy Kalish

If you don't pay attention to any section other than this one, you will still have learned a lot. Self esteem and a woman's orgasm — let's just say if you were trying to make ice cream instead of love, self esteem would be the equivalent of milk. And, it would not only be an ingredient, it would be the MAIN ingredient.

Since we've already talked about a woman's role in society, how about mentioning what the perfect woman is suppose to look like. Take a look at the front of any magazine stand and I will guarantee the cover pages will be filled with people who fall into the "I am perfect, beautiful, and weigh 120 pounds while wet" category. That is a pretty hard category to measure up to. Unless a woman has total confidence in her body, she is self-conscious when naked. Even if your partner falls into a slender category, that doesn't necessarily mean that she is not self-conscious. She still has her breasts to think about, she still has firmness to think about and she most likely still does not look like a cover girl in the morning.

One of the biggest inhibitions women have about sex is the way they look. How can they not? The most popular magazine that men subscribe to is *Playboy*. How many *Playboy* pictorials have overweight women? None. Try to live up to that. Women are up against models who base their whole life on taking care of their bodies and good looks because they are being paid. They are up against breast implants, a full time make-up artist and a lot of airbrushing. Women also know that's what you like to see and what you like to look at; and that's why *Playboy* is so popular.

When a woman falls short of what she considers to be your expectations, it's heart-wrenching to say the least. If she is uncomfortable with her body and she thinks her partner is not attracted to her body, sexual tensions run high. How many women have you ever known who like to have sex with the lights on? It is not because they're afraid of the light, it's because they're afraid of their body — afraid you will see their imperfections in the light and that you won't be sexually stimulated by them. Imagine having all of this running through

40

your head while also concentrating on having an orgasm; it can't happen.

A friend once told me that through her first marriage, which lasted six years, she would never make love outside of the covers because she didn't want her husband to have to look at her body. She always told him she was just shy and she liked sex better in the dark, under the covers. BIG WHITE LIE! She probably would have loved sex anywhere — on the kitchen counter, in the living room or on the floor, and in bright lights — had she felt comfortable with herself. She was missing wonderful sexual experiences because of her own insecurities.

This is a big problem but not something you can't change. A compassionate partner can practically move mountains if needed. First off you must decide if your partner is pleasing to your eyes. Does looking at your partner sexually excite you? If it does, you need to let her know and let her know often. Usually when you are working with a woman with low self-esteem, you are fighting a strong conviction that she has had for a long time; changing it takes patience and time.

Here are some good ideas to help rid her of her inhibitions:

1. *Start with candlelight and tell her how much looking at her body turns you on, how sexy she looks, how perfect her breasts are and how beautiful she is.*

2. *Request a private strip show; tell her the thought of watching her undress for you makes you crazy!*

3. *Ask for your own private photo; tell her you need to be able to look at her naked body when she's not around (and of course you would be the only person who would see the photo).*

4. *Have sex in front of mirrors. Help her explore her body in front of the mirrors and tell her how perfect each and every part is and how excited looking at her gets you.*

5. *Buy her revealing lingerie and ask her to model it for you while, once again, verbally confirming her beauty. Learn to compliment her not only during sexual experiences, but also throughout the day.*

I once had a boyfriend who I would catch staring at me for no particular reason while I was reading or when I was watching television. When I would ask what he was staring at he would answer, "I'm just looking at how beautiful you are." That is probably the best thing anyone has ever said to me. I don't think he even realized it at the time, but the feeling those words gave me inside were irreplaceable and will always stand out in my mind. It is amazing how much pleasure you can give someone with words.

For those of you who are not so pleased with the way your partner looks, stick with the old saying, "If you can't say something nice, don't say it at all." I am not telling you to lie; I don't think lying for any reason in a relationship is good. I am saying do not insult or demean her. If the sight of your partner does not sexually excite you, it's time for you to re-evaluate your relationship and see how much you truly love her. I am a firm believer in "If you love the inside, you can't help but love the outside." It goes hand in hand. If you love your partner and want to keep your relationship, but her weight is a concern to you, help her with it. Although I don't know any women out there who like to be overweight, I do know it is a hard struggle and that if you have two people working at it instead of one it helps a lot.

Here are some ideas:

1. *Tell her you want to get into better shape and you are going to start going to the gym. Ask if she would like to come along and give you some company.*

2. *Ask her to go for a quite romantic walk with you after dinner.*

3. *Buy a waverunner for the family (great exercise!).*

4. *Buy his and her rollarblades.*

5. *Volunteer to cook dinner (cook low-cal).*

6. *Make your next vacation a health resort.*

7. *Stop at a market on a weekly basis and bring home fresh fruit.*

8. *Take her out dancing. Encourage her and praise her efforts.*

You might be thinking that a woman should be responsible for her own weight loss, but if it is something bothering both of you, then both of you should be united in a solution. And, does it really ever hurt to have a little help from someone? The important point to remember is criticism doesn't work. It never has. It never will. As a matter of fact, it usually brings on an opposite reaction. If a person is told that she is overweight and undesirable it brings on a feeling of hopelessness and rejection. The second to last thing she'll want to do is diet, and the last thing she'll want to do is have sex with the person who is criticizing her.

Sex, love, compassion, tenderness, patience and caring all go together. In case you read over that list too fast the first time: *sex, love, compassion, tenderness, patience,* and *caring* all go together!

Sometimes a woman has not looked deep enough inside herself to find the reason she isn't achieving sexual fulfillment. Maybe your partner knows she has low self-esteem but she hasn't connected it with her sex life and doesn't know on a sub-conscious level it is affecting her. I believe that any woman who is inhibited about her body is not living up to the sexual pleasures she can have.

The easiest way to tell if your partner has low self-esteem is to pay attention. Pay attention to the way she acts in the bedroom. Does she exhibit her body to you? Does she like the lights on during sex acts? Does she walk around the room naked after sex or go straight for the first robe she can find to cover herself? Does she complain about her weight or her breast size? These are all common acts of a woman with low self-esteem. Just helping her feel better about her body can give her the inspiration to start having uninhibited passionate sex. What could be better?

● ● ●

44

THE MALE EGO

"Women fake orgasm if they really care about the man because they don't want him to feel a sense of failure."
—Annie Flanders

I have talked a little about what inhibits a woman from having an orgasm, but why is it she not only doesn't have orgasms, but she looks at you, smiles and says she did? Easy — because of the male ego. Believe it or not, one of the biggest compliments a woman can give you is faking an orgasm. Stick with me here — when a woman fakes an orgasm she is giving up her right to pleasure in order for you to feel good about yourself, so no feelings are hurt.

Imagine you just had two hours of unbridled passionate sex. You have worked up a sweat, the sheets have been ripped off and the beds and the candles are melted to a stub. You are feeling pretty good about yourself. You have orgasmed two, maybe three times, in the last two hours, and you look over at your partner with that spark in your eye and ask, "Was it good for you?" She looks over with the sweat still gleaming on her body and says, "Nope."

So where are you now? You're in the land of devastation, that's where. And most women know this so, instead of telling you the truth, they do the itsy bitsy white lie trick: "Oh my God, was it good." "Where did you learn how to do that?" "You know how to satisfy me better than anyone." "You are the best lover I have ever had." "I have never had so many orgasms at one time." The lines could go on and on.

So you see, women who fake orgasms are giving the ultimate sacrifice. They not only help you achieve orgasm; they watch you have an orgasm. And then, with no satisfaction of their own, tell you how satisfying you are, so that you not only have a satisfied body, you now have a satisfied ego to match.

Bernie Zilbergeld, author of *The New Male Sexuality,* says it best: "The male ego rests on the twin pillars of money and sex. Men believe they should know how to make money and how to make love. Admitting they could learn something about sex from a woman is hard because they don't feel like 'real' men unless they are competent lovers."

Men believe that they should instinctively know how to pleasure a woman. And, any input to the contrary can be a devastating blow to the ego. How brave, or should I ask, how callous, does one have to be to inflict that kind of harsh reality on a man? Many women feel it would not only hurt your feelings, but the repercussions of being too honest could be detrimental to your sex life. Why go through all that when you can just lie a little and make your partner feel like a sex god?

Another reason a woman might fake an orgasm is that, if she has been faking for years and years, any honesty now would be her admitting she did not just tell one lie or stretch the truth a little; she lied over and over and continually deceived you. This is something nobody would want to hurry up and admit.

If your partner fakes an orgasm, more than likely, the snowball effect began right after your first sexual experience. Many women believe the first sexual experience is not the time to bring up any sexual dissatisfaction and really neither is the second because you're still in a new, delicate relationship. Then there's the third and forth, and so on, until the next thing she knows, she feels like a pathological liar and doesn't want to admit it. It's one of those woman things you take to your grave.

Another fear women have is the fear of the unknown. How are you going to react? What are you going to say? Will you be mad? Will you never want to have sex again? Will it bruise your ego so bad that you will stop having sex altogether? Will you want to go out and find someone else who might enjoy you sexually? There is a lot of fear that has to be overcome before a woman can be confident enough to tell you how she feels about your sexual relations.

Wouldn't it be great to know exactly what your partner is thinking — to know if you are really satisfying her? Of course it would, and of course you can. Here we go again with that word "communication." If you can effectively communicate with your partner then she will be able to effectively communicate with you. You need to go into the conversation with the mentality of a woman. You are starting to learn how women think and feel, now is the time to act on it.

You need to start any conversations about sex with the expectation that your partner does, on occasion, fake an orgasm. You need to know this before you even begin talking. You also need to express that you might know why. It would even be a good idea to read this chapter over with her. Tell her you won't be mad and you won't have your feelings hurt if she is faking, and that she has put her sexual satisfaction on hold long enough. Together, both of you can work through it. If you explain this in a truly understanding way, she is more likely to be honest enough to open up to you.

Unfortunately, her fears may be so deeply rooted that even after confronting her with your newfound knowledge she still might not be so willing to admit it. Keep in mind two things: first, if she is not sexually satisfied she doesn't necessarily have to admit it for you to change the situation; and second, maybe after changing the way you stimulate her mentally and physically, she will eventually open up. Sometimes it's easier to admit something in the past tense such as, "I used to fake having an orgasm but in the last two years I haven't."

I would officially like to welcome you to the world of women. Faking an orgasm has been a common secret bond among women for years — a secret most women know and share with other women but which few admit to their partners. This is your chance to go where few men have gone — into the deepest part of the sexual woman.

● ● ●

THE FEMALE EGO

"Women have tolerated miserable relationships, faked orgasm, and generally kept quiet about their needs, all in the name of romantic love."
—Eleanor Stephans

So now that we've talked about the male ego, what about the other side of the coin? One of the contributing factors to why women fake an orgasm is not only the male ego, but their own ego as well. Many women believe that if they are not enjoying sex to the fullest extent that there is something wrong with them. If their partner is doing everything right in the bedroom, why are they still not having an orgasm? They feel that they are defective in some way and do not want to admit it. Or, they think that since it is "their problem" it won't do any good communicating it to you. After all, if they have the sexual dysfunction, what can you do to help? That's where the communication stops.

This ego problem is so severe that I have had close friends lie about how great their partner was in the bedroom and how many times they had orgasmed, only to find out years later that they weren't satisfied. Again, it's one of those past tense things..."I never used to orgasm when having sex, now I've finally found out what I was missing."

Why have I never confronted anyone with the fact that they used to brag about how great their sex life was? Because, it's painfully obvious why someone would lie. Who wants to admit they don't have the best sex life? Who wants people to feel sorry for them or think that something is either wrong with them physically or emotionally? Who wants their friends looking at their partner and knowing he is not satisfying? It's just simply easier to lie.

Another fear she might have is that by expressing any sexual frustration she has, she might be compared to your former partners, who did enjoy themselves sexually. What men and women do not realize is that faking an orgasm is more common than they might think.

One of the worst things that can happen to a woman who has finally broken through her fears about communicating her sexual dissatisfaction, is to be met by a partner who takes no responsibility and blames it on her. "Well, my ex-wife didn't ever have a problem having an orgasm, something must be wrong with you" or "My last girlfriend said I was the best lover she ever had, I don't know why you're having a problem."

Placing blame can be a quick response when a man feels like his sexuality is being threatened. Before you are so quick to judge, keep this in mind: If your partner is having problems achieving an orgasm (that are not physically related, which few are), more than likely, so has every girl you have ever been with. None were honest and straight-forward enough to tell you.

Although it may not be your first instinct, you should be grateful and thankful if your partner opens up to you and actually communicates any dissatisfaction she may have. Do not think of this as an insult, think of it as an opportunity to grow and enrich your sex life.

After reading this you have to realize how many fears she has set aside to be honest with you. Remember the old saying: "You can't fix something, unless you know it's broken." What a great way to start improving and growing in your sexual experiences! I believe that honesty and open communication are the best things that can ever happen to two people. Once you achieve them your sexual relationship, as well as your relationship as a whole, will be better than ever.

● ● ●

SEXUAL BACKGROUND

"Great sex is between two people, not just two bodies. It is an understanding of the other person..."
—Alexandra Penney

Abuse

Statistics reveal that one out of every four women have been sexually abused, molested or raped at some time in their life. This can cause more than just a little strain on your sex life. Research has shown that one of the greatest effects of rape is difficulty becoming sexually aroused. A female who has been sexually abused may fear men, fear intimacy, may feel unworthy or feel embarrassed. Even though the abuse is in the past tense, the fear and emotions can stay with a woman for a lifetime.

Your partner may be too embarrassed to tell you if she has experienced sexual abuse. Many times women are not only ashamed of the fact they were abused; they are also ashamed of themselves for being abused. If your partner has told you or you have reason to believe she has been abused, it is important that you consider counseling. Left untreated, the effects of sexual abuse can be devastating to a relationship.

This situation can be frustrating to a man, especially if it is effecting your sexual relationship. You might think you understand how horrible her situation is even though you did not create it and are the one being punished by her lack of intimacy. And, you might feel it unfair that you have to deal with the problem. Well it is unfair, but it is just as unfair that she has had to deal with it.

The healing process associated with any traumatic experience takes time and patience. If your partner has been sexually abused more than likely she cannot "get over it" or "just forget about it" without additional help. And, since any sexual problems she might be having effect both of you, together you need to work on solving them.

There is no "quick fix" available when dealing with sexual abuse. However, there are many counselors who specialize in sexual abuse who can provide the information needed to overcome any problems you may be facing.

Since I am not a counselor I cannot tell you in detail how to cure any sexual problems that may arise from rape or abuse. But, as a woman, I can tell you that this is a situation when your partner needs you more than ever. She needs all your understanding, love and patience to help renew her self-worth.

I have said over and over how important mental stimulation is to a woman. Now is the time to utilize your knowledge on self-esteem practices, to provide gentleness and kindness, and unconditional affection. With the help of qualified counselors and a loving partner, any woman can learn to experience true sexual pleasure, sexual intimacy and orgasm.

Religious beliefs

More than likely, any person with a religious background has been raised to believe that sex before marriage is wrong and that it is a sin punishable by God.

I am not saying that it is right or wrong, however, I would like to say that the majority of religions that teach how horrible sex is before marriage tend to leave out how beautiful sex is after marriage. I have never heard of a church that preaches about how wonderful sex can be. My point being, after years of growing up hearing how wrong and sinful sex is, a woman facing her sexuality may feel as if she is completely going against everything she has been taught throughout her lifetime.

Many people do not realize how much of an affect this can have on a child or teenager when growing up. Since people fail to mention all the gratifying aspects of sex — it makes you feel wonderful, it brings you closer to your partner, and it can be the most pleasant experience you ever have — it tends not to be an expectation in adult life.

According to *Sex and Morality in the U.S.*, when asked to remember some of their earliest sexual experiences, 33.2% of women felt very strong feelings of guilt, shame or embarrassment. For some reason, this particular guilt tends to have a larger affect on women. It can affect her sexuality in many ways — her beliefs on masturbation, fantasies, fetishes, oral sex, etc. Any guilt on a conscious or unconscious level can conflict with a quality sexual experience. Your partner will not be able to enjoy sex and openly receive pleasure if she believes it to be wrong.

My own personal belief is that sex is not sinful if you are with someone you love and are in a monogamous relationship, but every woman's beliefs will not be the same. Some women do not think sex is sinful at all, some think sex before marriage is wrong, and some believe oral sex is wrong. Religious beliefs and backgrounds on sex can run the gamut. What is important is that her beliefs are not interfering with your mutual pleasure.

If your partner has inhibitions which stem from guilt or religious beliefs, it is important to communicate your concerns and try to reach a compromise. If this fails, I would suggest seeking a qualified sex therapist. The most detrimental belief that can affect her pleasure is the belief that it is wrong for her to experience pleasure.

● ● ●

PAIN vs. PLEASURE

"Macho doesn't prove mucho."
—Zsa Zsa Gabor

There are times when sex might be so extremely painful for a woman, that she fakes an orgasm just to finish every thing up. The thought process that goes along with painful sex is something like: "I am in pain and I want the pain to go away, so maybe if I fake an orgasm he will hurry up and get this over with and my pain will go away." Sounds like great sex, huh?

I would say that almost all women at one time in their life have faked an orgasm for exactly this reason. And, what a horrible reason to have to fake. The really sad thing is that the majority of these situations are not medically related. Pain is usually caused by one of two things: either an inexperienced partner or what I refer to as "the macho lover."

An inexperienced partner typically does not give enough foreplay or hasn't learned what buttons to push to excite his partner. When a female is excited and ready for sex she releases fluid from her vagina or, as men would say, "She gets really wet." (This is not always true for older females. See lesson 7, Sex and the Senior.) This fluid has been created for a reason, it is necessary for pleasurable sex.

Some men seem to think that if she's wet it helps the situation, but it is not necessary. Or, worse yet, they think if they can just get it in she will get wet sooner or later. Let's clarify this. Sex should not be painful, not even for the first minute. If you are serious about satisfying your partner, you have to make sure what you are doing feels good.

If you have any question in your mind about whether or not you have spent enough time with foreplay, don't worry, she has a built in foreplay meter. If she's really wet you have given enough foreplay. If she's not, you still have work to do. See how easy this is?

Now let's talk about "the macho lover," which I do believe there's a little of in every man. The "macho lover" gets excited when he conquers. Here's an example: You have your partner bent over the bed. You enter her, going slowly at first and then picking up the pace. You notice her moans are turning into slight screams and her knuckles are white from grabbing the blankets. She says "it's too deep" or "easy" or something that let's you know it is slightly painful for her. Do you ease up? Or, do you get a "macho lover" attitude — "I have a big penis and it can hurt!"

What is this? Some male ego thing? Why is it that some men don't understand pain is bad? Since I'm not a man, I don't understand what kind of ritual practice this is, but I know first hand that it happens. And, it happens a lot. The surest way to get a man to increase his sexual intensity is to verbally express discomfort. For some reason, statements of discomfort are interpreted as "Harder, harder, let me writhe in pain from your manhood."

The reason I call it "the macho lover" routine is because, after it is all said and done, they generally turn to the woman with a look of beaming pride and say, "Oh, I'm sorry. Did I hurt you?" Macho men want to have a powerful penis — powerful enough to drill a hole in concrete. If you are a macho lover, let me put your ego at ease: You do have a powerful penis and it can inflict very much pain — no need to try to prove it anymore.

The quickest way to induce a faked orgasm is through discomfort; it will work every time. Any woman will fake an orgasm in an instant to avoid enduring a painful experience. And, the easiest part is that they don't have to do a lot of faking. They are already screaming or moaning loudly due to the pain, now all they have to add is the verbal "I'm coming" to get it over with.

This is the absolute worst reason for faking that a woman can inflict upon herself and her partner. Because, after it's all over, you are probably thinking, "Wow, I can't believe the way she reacted! She was screaming and moaning — she loved it! I will have to remember to do it just like that more often."

Unfortunately, many men are not aware that this is not the way to bring a woman to orgasm. They learn their sexual techniques by what they hear and see and, unfortunately, if you have ever watched a porno movie, many times they show hard, painful sex to be exciting to a woman. These movies are extremely misleading. The majority of viewers for these types of movies are men and the people who produce them know that. In turn, they give you what you want to see and not necessarily what excites a woman. Unless your partner is into sadomasochism, please know this to be truth: To bring a woman to orgasm, she needs a pleasurable, not painful, experience.

● ● ●

lesson

4

"Men today presumably know how women feel about foreplay. Yet to read some of the Cosmo *women complaints, it would appear that men often ignore or overlook what they know."*
—Linda Wolfe

The main questions men seem to need answered about foreplay are: What is considered foreplay? How long should it last? And how important is it? Let's start with the first question.

What is considered foreplay?

There are two types of foreplay and both are needed to produce extreme sexual pleasure. The first type of foreplay is "general foreplay." General foreplay is the little things you do throughout the day that bring a closeness and intimacy between you and your partner. General foreplay is a major factor in bringing desire into your relationship.

Hugs, kisses, communication, touches, loving looks and gentle words are all forms of general foreplay. Many men are under the delusion that foreplay is the fifteen minute time period before the actual sex act. They fail to understand that the daily emotions and feelings a woman has directly influences her sex drive and her sexual enjoyment. There needs to be a building of anticipation throughout the day to provide a passion for the sex at night.

General foreplay, if done right, starts the moment you wake up in the morning. One sentence such as, "I can't wait till I get back from work so I can make love to you all night," is considered general foreplay. Coming back into the house because you have forgotten to give your partner a kiss goodbye is also considered general foreplay. Giving your partner a massage, holding hands, going for walks together, getting double-decker ice cream cones on a hot night, reading to each other, and watching movies curled up on the same couch together, is foreplay, too. Get the picture? Anything that you do that is romantic, sensual or loving, is considered general foreplay and is as important as sexual foreplay!

It is about the feelings that two people share with each other on a daily basis that makes them want to have sex with one another. It is what makes you appealing to women and what makes them feel appealing to you. In a word, it is *romantic*, which you should know by now is important in any sexual relationship. Be romantic, be spontaneous, be creative and be loving, and you will always be an expert at "general foreplay."

The second type of foreplay is "sexual foreplay." Unlike general foreplay, sexual foreplay requires a physical closeness with your partner. It is the caressing, touching, fondling, nibbling and exploring of a woman's body. For a woman, quality sexual foreplay can be as exciting and stimulating as the sex act itself.

Sexual foreplay can also be a valuable learning tool. Because every woman has different erogenous zones, sexual foreplay gives you the opportunity to explore your partners body and find out what pleasures her.

How long should it last?

Sexual foreplay can last between hours and minutes depending on the circumstances. Keep in mind that this type of exploration can be extremely pleasurable and exciting, so it is a good idea to take your time and enjoy.

It is also important to remember that if there hasn't been a sufficient amount of foreplay, your partner may not be physically ready for sex; she hasn't produced enough natural lubrication. And as I have mentioned, this can cause uncomfortable sex, and uncomfortable sex is not pleasurable sex. This is not to say an excessive amount of foreplay is always needed. There may be different times in your sexual encounters when your partner may need little to no sexual foreplay. A good example of this is quickies. Her excitement level may peak quickly due to anticipation, in which case minimal sexual foreplay is needed.

It is extremely important to correctly read your partner's natural body signals. If you have any doubts about your intuition, just ask her. With quality communication you can learn enough about her body and desires, that you will no longer have to ask.

How important is foreplay?

Other than the exception of the occasional quickie, foreplay is extremely important. Lack of foreplay is the most common mistake made in a sexual relationship. And, I firmly believe that this is the main reason women do not achieve orgasm as often as men.

Most women require a great amount of foreplay. For them, foreplay creates a mental readiness. And since we know that a woman's largest erogenous zone is her mind, quality foreplay is a necessity to quality sex.

Since men and women have such obvious differences in their need for foreplay, I thought it might be easier to explain with analogies most men can understand.

For a woman, sex without foreplay is like...

- Only getting to watch the last fifteen minutes of a football game to see who wins or loses.

- Having to start your golf game on the putting green of the ninth hole.

- Having hockey tickets that only allow you in the game during the third period.

- Going for your six pack of beer in the refrigerator and finding the first five gone.

Hopefully that paints a good picture. For most things in life, the events that precede the ending are just as, if not more important than the ending itself. Sex is no exception.

Now that you know the basics about foreplay, it's time to get into the specifics. In the following lesson you will learn the "how to's" of foreplay. This information will provide you with many great ideas to enhance your foreplay techniques. And, now that you know how important foreplay is, you definitely need to become an expert.

● ● ●

COMMUNICATION

"Ultimately, the bond of all companionship, whether in marriage or friendship, is conversation."
—Oscar Wilde

As I am writing this I can already hear the moans and groans of the many men reading this title. As unsettling as it may be, communication is the key ingredient to a quality sex life. I am sure you may have already noticed that in every lesson the word "communication" was used. The only reason it was so frequently used is because it is so frequently needed; there's no getting around it.

Without communication, you cannot effectively convey your wants and desires. You have to become a mind reader and there are very few people qualified for that position. This lesson will provide you with different techniques useful in effective communication. I am hoping that after discovering how simple it can be, it might help to ease the discomfort communication usually inflicts on men.

Most sex therapists suggest that the most common problem couples have in their relationship is the lack of communication. That does not necessarily mean they are not talking, they are just not communicating — big difference. There are three main reasons for poor communication: hearing, but not listening; talking, but not properly conveying; and, the worst, not speaking at all. The following are suggestions for quality communication:

Listening

To effectively listen you have to keep an open mind and give your partner your undivided attention. You should not interrupt, jump to conclusions or make hasty judgments. You should ask questions and consider your partner's statements before responding.

Speaking

First and most importantly, you must talk. Bring your words from your heart and your head, and not from your emotions. Emotions can change from one minute to the next. If you are mad about something, do not let it ruin your conversation — more than likely you will end up saying things you will regret.

Do not build up a wall of silence. If you are dissatisfied, say something. And, to keep an even flow of communication, when you are satisfied, say something. Too often the only time people attempt to communicate is when they are arguing. It is no surprise that under these circumstances people have trouble with effective communication.

Since I began this book almost every close male friend of mine has found it necessary to call and ask different sexual or relationship questions. I have never minded giving them honest straightforward answers, but I always end the conversations with, "Why are you asking me and not your partner?" It seems many men are curious and want to talk but are uncomfortable talking with their partner.

This can be the ruin of a relationship. There has to be quality communication for quality sex. Throughout this book I can provide you with basic information to enhance your sex life, but what I cannot do is tell you the specific likes and dislikes of your partner. There is not a book out there that can. If you do not discuss your sexual preferences with your partner you will never know if she is satisfied.

That is the main reason I placed this topic in the foreplay lesson. It is necessary for you to be able to discuss the different techniques mentioned before trying them. Both of you need to know what techniques you are comfortable with, which ones you enjoyed, which ones you didn't, etc. These are insights you can't just guess, you need communication.

I am sure you have practiced effective communication at one point or another in time. Most couples, when they first meet, spend much of their time talking and discovering each other. Unfortunately, as the relationship progresses, the communication slowly diminishes. If you have lost communication in your relationship, it is time to bring it back.

If your conversation falls on deaf ears or she doesn't feel comfortable discussing her sexual preferences, keep trying. In

63

lesson eight you will find a questionnaire specifically designed to create a sexual conversation; try using it to break the ice. Do not wait for your partner to initiate sexual conversations; start them and then ask for her input. Many times people are less embarrassed talking about certain subjects if their partner has openly discussed them first.

Because I am aware that many men would rather have their fingernails pulled out than sit down and communicate with their partner, I honestly wish I could have skipped this subject and moved on to the more preferable hands-on lessons. There was just no way of getting around it. To my knowledge, the only way to achieve a quality sexual relationship is through communication. I am, however, extremely confident that once you see the many rewards effective communication can bring to your sex life, you will want to talk — a lot.

● ● ●

THE FIVE SENSES

"Women are on the whole more sensual than sexual, men are more sexual than sensual."
—Mai Zelterling

The first time I achieved orgasm with a partner was years after my first sexual encounter. After being in a long-term sexual relationship I honestly did not believe I could have an orgasm. I was doing everything right, or so I thought, and my partner was doing everything right, or so he thought, so what was wrong? I had to wait years later for my third partner to teach me how to achieve orgasm. Don't get me wrong, I don't believe all of it was because of him, I did have a lot of time to get comfortable with my own body and learn about what was pleasurable to me. But looking back, he had as much control on my ability to orgasm as I did.

What was so special about him? After comparing his sexual practices with my previous partners I decided the main difference was in his foreplay. He was the epitome of sex. Every part about him was sexual, not in a disgusting, vulgar way, but in a gentle, sensual way (there is a big difference). Sometimes, when he would look at me, I could tell instinctively by his look that he was thinking about what he was going to do to me later. This kind of look was enough to give me goose bumps from head to toe. And when I was going to have sex with him, I knew it. He attacked all five of my senses, and completely overwhelmed them with sexuality. It took any and all mental distractions away.

Since this seemed to work for him and it definitely worked for me, I am going to share a few of his secrets. I don't think he would even consider them secrets, that is just the way he was — and what a way to be!

What do I mean by attacking the five senses? Well, first let's go over them. Touching, tasting, smelling, seeing and hearing are needed with ambiance to bring them all together.

Touch

Let's get basic. Soft, gentle caresses are good. Groping, pulling, overpowering is bad. I want you to think about the difference between sandpaper and soft velvet — which would you prefer to have run across your body before sex? Other than men who are into sadomasochism, I believe most would prefer velvet. Women are the same — the softer, the gentler, the better. And, where do you touch? Everywhere!

Contrary to what many men believe, a woman has more than two erogenous zones. A woman's entire body is an erogenous zone — shoulders, stomach, thighs, calves, the small of her back, her fingers, her ankles, her sides, etc. I'm sure you get my point. Every inch on a woman's body is sensitive and can get her sexually aroused.

As a matter of fact, the longer you stay away from the nipples and clitoris, the more the anticipation builds. Besides, where's the fire? Bonus Hint: When trying to build anticipation, gently brush pass her clitoris or kiss her nipples for a moment and then move on to a different area. This will make her crazy with excitement.

Slowly linger and explore a woman's body. Touch her body gently with feathers or satin sheets, or massage her with warmed creams, lotions or oils. Kiss her entire body and overwhelm her sense of touch.

When overwhelming the senses, what you are trying to accomplish is, deleting any and all distractions. Because of this, you want to think about the little things: Is your belt buckle stabbing her in the stomach? Are you being too rough (like sandpaper). Is she lying in a comfortable area and in a comfortable position? When in the realms of passion, you do not want a woman thinking, "His five o'clock shadow feels like it is going to rub a hole into my skin." This would be considered a distraction. You want her entire sense of feel to be *"feel good."*

Taste

This is as simple as "touch." How about some of her favorite wine or, for that matter, her favorite drink? Another good idea is to take a drink of something, hold it in your mouth and then release it into her mouth while kissing. That is sexy, sexy, sexy!

Don't worry if you spill any, you can use your tongue to gently wipe it up.

How about hand feeding her juicy ripe strawberries or grapes, or small pieces of cake with icing to lick off of your fingers. Drizzle small amounts of honey in her mouth and continue running it over her body for you to lick off — there's also a lot to be said for chocolate syrup. Let your imagination run wild. In the movie *9 1/2 Weeks*, there is a part in it where Mickey Rourke puts a blind fold on Kim Bassinger and feeds her different types of food — this is extremely erotic. It's worth a watch if you have never seen it. Food is not a requirement for stimulating her sense of taste, but always having something good to drink is a plus.

Smell

Well, I want to go over the obvious first, no bad breath – it's far from sexy. Shower — body odor can be a distraction. Actually, let me clarify that one: There is an odor that a man can get when sweating, not an overwhelming body odor, but more of a musky, masculine type of scent, which at times can be very appealing.

You want to be careful not to overwhelm her sense of smell with overpowering aftershave or cologne. You want it to be a soft, pleasant, appealing smell. Scented candles work well for this, as do massage oils. Also, a wood burning fireplace always smells good in the winter. Once again, your main objective is to overcome any distractions.

You don't want your partner thinking: "Wow, he's great in bed, but boy do his feet stink!"

Your new mantra is *"no distractions."*

Sight

And what would you like your partner to see? This is where we go back to the multi-purpose low lighting candles, so she can watch what you are doing to her. Gazing into her eyes is also a wonderful experience for a woman. The key here is to take advantage of every circumstance you have. For example, if you have a street light that shines into your window at night, crack open the blinds. If it is dark inside, no one can see in. It creates a streaked light effect which when reflected on a body can be very sensual. (O.K., watching "9 1/2 Weeks" is a must.) Fireplace light is also a good idea. How about making love outside with the stars as your backdrop?

Take advantage if you are on vacation. Always get a room with a view. There is nothing more romantic than having a view of the snow topped mountains of Colorado while making love; the lights of Las Vegas or Atlantic City, from high in a hotel room; or an ocean view in Cancun. Even those cheesy, red motel lights have their own kind of sexual ambiance when shining through a window.

Sound

There are many great ideas that fall into this category. Your own voice is one — having your partner whisper their sexual intentions for you is very erotic. In case you have never verbalized your intention before, the variations range from the tame, *"I want to make you feel so good tonight,"* *"You are so sexy,"* *"You are so beautiful,"* *"I love you,"* etc., to the more erotic, *"I am going to make love to you all night"* and *"I want to lick you all over."* You might already be thinking a lot of those thoughts, so don't be afraid to verbalize them. Moans and groans can also be a big turn-on.

You can get as detailed and as nasty as you and your partner feel comfortable with, but make sure both of you are comfortable with what you are saying. Some women get offended when you use obscene terms and phrases. The only way to find out what your partner likes without asking is to watch the way she responds. Does she talk back to you and use those same words? Ask her if talking dirty to her turns her on.

Music is also a great aphrodisiac. There are multitudes of great sensual sounds, some of my favorites artists are:

Jazz:	Pat Methany, Tangerine Dream
New Age:	Enya and Enigma, Sounds of the Ocean, or Thunderstorms.
Oldies:	Frank Sinatra, Dean Martin, Barry Manilow, Vic Damone
Rock:	Joe Satriani, Genesis, Peter Gabrial, The Cure
R&B:	Prince, Janet Jackson, Boyz 2 Men, Barry White, Luther Vandross
Soft Rock:	Sade, Christopher Cross, Natalie Merchant, Sarah McLaughlin, Michael Bolton

This is the time when a multiple disc CD player comes in handy. With so many selections available you can find many CD's to meet a romantic criteria. Remember, the softer the better. This is not the time to pull out any Motley Crue tapes you might have lying around.

Ambiance

First off, no children — get grandma to take the kids for the night. You don't want all of your effort to be spoiled by a knock on your bedroom door. Children can be a big distraction: Can they hear us? Are we being too loud? On a special occasion, when you just want a night of unbridled wild sex, it's time for a babysitter. Also, make sure to turn the phone ringer off and turn all pagers in the household off — the president is not going to call and who else can't wait a couple of hours? Ringing phones and pagers going off do not have a place in the ambiance section.

Do not feel like you have to go overboard with this, or try to overwork it. Sex should be natural and not rehearsed. The purpose of this lesson is not to tell you your next sexual experience should be on top of the Eiffel tower with a string quartet, a full banquet, and a bed of hand picked rose petals — just try to achieve the same effect through being natural and romantic.

Stimulating all five senses should not be hard work. Let me give you an example: Imagine you and your partner leave all children and phones at home and take a soft blanket and a bottle of wine to the beach. Taste = wine. Sight = the ocean. Sound= the waves and you whispering sweet nothings in her ear. Touch = a soft blanket and the breeze from the ocean. Smell = clean, fresh air. By grabbing a blanket, some wine and taking a stroll to the beach, you have stimulated all five senses. You can get as elaborate or as simple as you want.

Another example: One scented candle and a bottle of ice water — how hard is that? Sight = you in candlelight. Sound = your moans. Touch = a comfortable bed. Taste = cool refreshing ice water. Smell = the scented candle. I do not want you to feel as if it is hard work to satisfy your partner. It should be creative, fun, relaxing and enjoyable for you both.

By stimulating all of a woman's senses simultaneously you have created an atmosphere which distractions cannot penetrate. She has no choice but to focus on her own sexual pleasure and pleasing you. You have enveloped her into a sensual world where pleasure is her only concern, and what a wonderful place to be.

● ● ●

MASTURBATION

"Don't knock masturbation. It is sex with somebody I love."
—Woody Allen

Whether it is because of guilt or shame, many people still do not talk about or admit they masturbate. Masturbation is the big taboo that no one talks about yet everyone does. Even some couples in long-term relationships feel uncomfortable disclosing their masturbation habits to each other. This is a form of inhibition and for a completely gratifying sexual experience to happen, there can be no inhibitions.

Masturbation can create a certain intimacy between two people. It's as if you're sharing your innermost secret. Many people have grown up believing masturbation is done alone behind closed doors, and is very secret and very private. If a woman can allow herself to share this secret, she is also allowing herself to break free of her inhibitions and release herself sexually.

71

It is also a very healthy and gratifying way to experience sex and it can be one of your greatest learning tools. When watching your partner masturbate, you can learn what pace your partner enjoys sex and what type of pressure to use. It is the ultimate nonverbal sexual communication.

Some people believe if they are married and have a steady sexual relationship there is no need for masturbation. What they don't realize is that masturbation can increase the intensity of an already passionate relationship. If you have never watched your partner masturbate, how can you be sure that you are manually stimulating her the way she likes?

For years, sex therapists have acknowledged the importance of masturbation. When therapists work with women who cannot achieve an orgasm, their treatment usually starts with advising their patients to masturbate manually or with the use of a vibrator. Because a lot of women are ignorant of their specific and often varying sexual needs, masturbation can help a woman distinguish exactly what pleasures her and where.

A safe and gratifying way to experience orgasm is with mutual masturbation. Both partners simultaneously masturbate while watching each other. This can be an extremely erotic experience for both participants. It is also a great way to break up the monotony of intercourse. If you have been in a long-term relationship, where you have only achieved an orgasm through oral sex or intercourse, mutual masturbation can be a new sensual alternative.

Some women are too embarrassed to masturbate in front of their partner. If your partner falls into this category, you can help her release her inhibitions. Start by touching her and then ask her how it feels: Should you apply more pressure or less?

Circular motions or up and down? Does it feel better with a lubricant? Gently persuade her to show you herself.

If your partner is inhibited about masturbation, ask her to try it a few times before she makes up her mind to never masturbate in front of you. Explain that you think it could be beneficial to your sex life and it will help you learn how to better please her. Remove all of her guilt and shame with words and if it helps, tell her you will masturbate for her first. Sometimes, once a woman has seen you have set your sexual inhibitions aside, so will she.

This might be a great erotic sight, but do not forget to pay attention. How is she moving and where is she concentrating her movements? Does she masturbate fast and with a passion, or slow and lingering? This is your educational show of exactly what she likes without her having to say a word — take advantage of it!

Don't be afraid to join in the fun! Kiss her body, play with her nipples, talk to her. Tell her how sexy she is, how great she looks and how excited you get when you watch her. Try to break down any lingering feelings of embarrassment or shame that she might have.

There are some women who are so set in their ways that either their inner guilt or embarrassment never allows them to fully appreciate the experience of masturbating with a partner. If, after trying, your partner is still uncomfortable practicing masturbation techniques, be understanding and maybe, after experiencing the other pleasures described in the coming lessons, she will become less inhibited. In time you can try it again.

Also, there are men who are intimidated by sex toys. They feel that if enjoyed enough, their partner might prefer the sex toy to them. Let me put your mind at ease. A vibrator, dildo or any other form of sexual aid can never replace the feelings a woman gets through human touch. It is exactly like when a male masturbates; it gets the job done. But, would you ever want it to replace sexual relations with a partner? Absolutely not. The enjoyment behind mutual masturbation is the mutual part — enjoying a new experience with a partner. Sexual aids can be used to enhance your sexual relationship, but they can never replace the real thing!

Sex should be fun, lighthearted and experimental. A good sexual relationship should always be creative and exciting. If you have never tried masturbation with a partner, it is a great way to increase passion and pleasure in your relationship.

There are hundreds of toys and sexual aids available to couples. The following is information you might find helpful when deciding on different products. Since there are so many different options for you to choose from, I am only going over the basic differences. If you and your partner have mutually agreed on purchasing sexual toys, it is better for both of you to participate in the selection. Just because you find a sex toy that is twelve inches long, spins in three directions and glows in the dark, does not necessarily mean your partner will find it enjoyable. Since it is going to be used on her body, she should have the final decision.

Dildos and Vibrators

The difference between a dildo and a vibrator is pretty simple: A vibrator vibrates and a dildo does not. I believe vibrators are more enjoyable for a woman. When using a vibrator she can concentrate the pulse on her clitoris to achieve orgasm. You will notice, although most vibrators are shaped like a penis, most women prefer to use the vibrator on their clitoris and rarely put it into their vagina. Since this is the case, there can be just as much satisfaction from a vibrating back massager, scalp massager, etc. These can be great options if you suffer from sex store phobia.

A dildo is mainly used for entering the vagina. Because of this, some other form of stimulation directed at her clitoris is needed to achieve orgasm. Not to say it cannot still get the results you want, you just have to work a little harder. Since there is not any direct contact with the clitoris, your partner will need to use both hands, one for the dildo and one to stimulate her clitoris manually. This is kind of like rubbing your head with one hand and your stomach with the other — awkward. This is where you come into play. You can help your partner by manually or orally stimulating her while she is using a dildo. If you are helping her manually, make sure you are not too rough and that it is pleasurable for her. A good suggestion is to ask her to show you first how she likes to be manually stimulated and then mimic her moves.

The old wive's tale of using a cucumber instead of vibrator is just that, an old wive's tale. Since a woman's most erogenous zone is on the outside of the vagina (the clitoris), a cucumber is not going to do a whole heck of a lot by itself. You might enjoy watching her use a vegetable on herself, but without your help, her enjoyment will be minimal at best. She needs direct clitoral stimulation. Any object you choose to use in place of a dildo should also include the additional clitoral stimulation described above.

I am sure there are many stores near you where you can purchase vibrators, dildos and other sex toys. However, if you would prefer mail order sent discreetly to your home, here are a few places you might find helpful: *Toys in Babeland,* 1-800-658-9119, www.babeland.com; *Good Vibrations,* 1-800-289-8423, goodvibe@well.com, www.goodvibe.com; or *Eves Garden,* 1-800-848-3837, www.evesgarden.com.

Lubricants

As with a man, lubricants can be very helpful when a woman masturbates, not just for vaginal entry, but also for clitoral stimulation. It is less abrasive for her and therefore can enhance the feelings she receives when she masturbates. There are many different sexual lubricants available. They range from a selection of flavored lubricants to lubricants that warm to the touch.

Baby oil or KY jelly are also good options. Baby oil also adds an extra benefit by doubling as a body glistener. What is more erotic than seeing a woman oiled down and masturbating for you? As I have said before, be creative. If you don't have baby oil handy, grab some vegetable oil, olive oil or anything else that can suit your need. If your partner has not been greatly excited by your current sexual relationship, start exciting her by adding new variations to your sexual practices.

If you intend to have intercourse with the use of a condom, be careful. Many condoms can not be used with lubricants such as baby oil. Make sure to check with your doctor or pharmacist to find out what lubricants are compatible. Many condom companies also have an 800 number available on their packaging to call with any questions.

Water Pressure

Water pressure can be an alternative to manual masturbation. According to *The Cosmo Report*, 28.3% of women who masturbated preferred using some form of water spray. This technique can vary from using a water massager to the faucet in the bathtub.

When using this specific form of stimulation, your partner needs to position herself where some form of water pressure has direct contact with her clitoris. Start out at a low pressure and then, at a comfortable level, slowly add to the intensity of the pressure. I would highly suggest starting out with a hand held water massager. Your partner might already be experiencing anxiety about masturbating in front of you. This is not the time to ask her to contort her body in order to accommodate the kitchen sink.

Masturbation For Him

Watching a man masturbate can also be an extremely erotic experience for a female. It can also help reduce her own inhibitions. By watching her partner masturbate, she can begin to see that it is a natural and normal act. If she can see that you do not have any sexual inhibitions about masturbation, it will be easier for her to let go of hers.

It can be a great learning experience for her also. When watching a man masturbate, a woman can see first hand (pardon the pun) exactly what he likes. Fast or slow, hard or soft, it is the same learning process a man experiences when watching a woman. If you have ever experienced problems communicating how and where you like to be touched, this is a great way to communicate with your partner without the use of words.

Pre-Ejaculation

Masturbation can also help any problems you might have with pre-ejaculation. If you practice masturbation to the point of orgasm and then stop before you orgasm, your body learns control. You can practice this technique until you reach the point in which you have total control of when you orgasm.

I would like to share with you another masturbation technique I learned from a past relationship. A boyfriend of mine would last unusually long when we were making love. Comparatively speaking, most men orgasm fairly quickly the first time and then the second time around last a little longer. There never seemed to be a quick first time with him. I complimented him once on his stamina and he revealed to me that he masturbated right before we saw each other so he could last longer when we were together.

I have always thought that was the most considerate act. He had actually planned ahead to make sure our lovemaking sessions were enjoyable and gratifying for me. That in itself let me know that my satisfaction was extremely important to him. I think it was a great idea and I believe it can be helpful for any man who has somewhat of a quick trigger.

● ● ●

EXPLORATION

"For lovers, touch is metamorphosis, all the parts of the body seem to change, and they become different and better."
—John Cheever

Many women believe that exploration, or petting, is the best part of foreplay. It can be used to discover stimulating areas and can be an extremely erotic experience. A problem that some women come across is that their partners tend to forget there are more than two erotic areas on a woman. A woman's body is covered with sensitive, erotic areas, some so under-explored that she might not even be aware of them.

Some examples of overlooked areas include the small of the back, the inside of the thighs, the neck, the stomach and the buttocks. Each woman is uniquely designed with her own erotic sensors; take the time to explore her body and find them.

Women will not only enjoy the physical sensations total body exploration can have, but also the mental advantages. When paying attention to the entire body you are sending the message that her whole body is important to you and not just the areas you find stimulating. In other words, you understand that there is an entire human being in bed with you and not just a set of breasts.

Be creative and imaginative. Some areas may only be sensitive to the lightest touch. Invest in a new feather duster or try using oils and lotions to add a variety of sensations. Talk with her as you touch her, ask her what specific areas feel good. One of my closest friends describes exploration with her husband as "a visit to a bad gynecologist." This is a prime example of lack of variety and definitely lack of communication. Do not fall into this unhealthy rut!

When it comes to exploring and touching the two most recognized erotic areas, the nipples and clitoris, it is a good idea to use an indirect touch. This will increase anticipation. The goal of foreplay is to put your partner in a situation where she always wants more. By ignoring or occasionally touching her clitoris and nipples you build an excitement that will increase her chance of having an orgasm.

When stimulating the clitoris, remember that it is very sensitive to touch. A common mistake made is to administer touch directly onto the clitoris. This is an understandable mistake because a woman does orgasm from clitoral stimulation. However, when a direct touch is used on a continual basis, it can have a painful effect. If you are not sure how your partner enjoys physical stimulation, ask her to show you. Or, if you are not comfortable with asking, gently guide her hand to her clitoris, watch and take mental notes.

Although the general idea of exploring a woman's body is to be gentle and not to inflict pain, an occasional squeeze or gentle bite can be highly erotic. Watch your partner's different body signals or ask her what she likes as you perform different techniques.

Because many women do not fully understand their own anatomy, especially if they do not participate in masturbation, they are frequently unable to enjoy sexual relations to the fullest extent. This is a problem that can be counteracted with a knowledgeable and experimental partner, one who takes the time to explore all of her body, and helps her discover and become aware of her erogenous areas.

So explore each other, use variety and continue to learn and grow. Human touch is essential to a quality relationship; it brings with it closeness, sensuality and knowledge. Your touch can be used in a playful, romantic or sensual way, but most importantly, it should be used.

● ● ●

lesson

5

SEX 101

"Sex is like money; only too much is enough."
—John Updike

This lesson will provide you with all of the information necessary for physically pleasuring a woman through basic sexual skills. I may call them basic because, as a woman, my wants and desires are innate — they may not be so basic for a man.

It is important to remember that sexual positions and techniques only have the ability to physically pleasure a woman. And, by now you should realize that although it is an important aspect in quality sex, the knowledge of different positions, turn-ons and techniques cannot provide a quality sexual experience unless you add mental and emotional stimulation. Once you have done that you will have mastered the art of pleasuring a woman.

TURN-ONS

"Desires are nourished by delays."
—Thomas Draxe

There are multitudes of different stimuli that can turn-on a woman. They can be broken down into two categories: mental, thoughts or fantasies, and physical stimulation. The one attribute they have in common is that the large majority of both mental and physical turn-ons involve anticipation.

When attempting to mentally turn a woman on, remember to use anticipation; never give away too much at one time. I have said many times throughout this book that anticipation brings on desire and want, and both of these feelings are what sexually stimulate a woman.

Another mental turn-on for most women is romance — rose petals leading to the bedroom, soft music on the radio, buying her a new sexy nightie, etc. Anything that requires a small amount of effort will make her feel important and desired. I am sure you will agree that knowing someone desires you is a big turn-on in itself.

Also, the feeling of being loved is a huge turn-on. Studies have shown that when a woman feels love from a man, her sexual life is generally more creative and more satisfying. This makes a lot of sense because, if you think about it, when a man really loves his partner, he is more likely to provide her with the romance and the mental stimulation she needs.

Although women are more mentally stimulated, there are also many physical ways to arouse them. According to *The Cosmo Report,* 95% of the women surveyed like their partner to undress them before sex. This directly reflects the desire many women have to be "taken." It is a non-verbal form of flattery, which implies that you are the pursuer and desire her so much you have to get her out of her clothes — now.

Some other forms of physical turn-ons include: anything soft; satin sheets; tender caresses; washing her in a long, hot bath; whispering sexy words; or just telling her how much you love her. Be creative and be gentle, and you cannot go wrong.

A large difference between men and women is their outlook on teasing. Some men believe that teasing is annoying or unnecessary. Women, on the other hand, not only desire to be teased, but because their arousal process is much slower than that of a man's, they physically need it. They need the time to build excitement in their body. Whether you are using mental stimulation or physical, always remember anticipation. That is one of a woman's biggest turn-on's.

● ● ●

POSITIONS

"If I was going to write a book about sex I would call it: Ow, You're On My Hair."
—Richard Lewis

Because many men are still under the mistaken belief that knowing and utilizing different sexual positions can make them a quality sexual partner, I would like to provide you with more realistic statistics.

How many women have regular orgasms as a result of intercourse?

Only 30% - *The Hite Report*
Only 34% - *The Cosmo Report*

How many women always have an orgasm during intercourse?

Only 15% - *Janus Report*
Only 29% - *Sex in America Survey*

This information further proves the idea that women need much more than the physical aspect of a relationship for a quality sex life.

Although there is no specific position that can guarantee orgasm for your partner, there are techniques that will increase the chances.

Woman Superior — This position has been reported to be the most successful in providing orgasm. It easily provides direct stimulation to the clitoris. When a woman is on top, she has the ability and control to maneuver her body into the exact position that brings her pleasure. She can regulate the amount of friction and rhythm in order to accommodate her specific needs. There is also evidence that shows men tend to last longer in this position.

Hint: When using this position your partner should try different levels, such as sitting straight up, with her legs bent on both sides of you, eventually moving down to a face to face position. Many times there is a very specific area which needs a certain amount of pressure for a woman to achieve an orgasm. Often, women move too quickly or do not

86

pay close attention to their own body and as a result believe that they can't orgasm during sex. A little time and a lot of patience can solve this problem.

Male Superior — Although this position is not as physically stimulating for a woman, surprisingly enough, it has been reported to be the favorite. This position provides closeness, intimacy and comfort. Many women prefer the male superior position because of the feelings of security it provides. And this position, by far, is the most romantic.

Hint: Confused about which position to choose? The favorite or the most stimulating? Try both in the same session. Start out with the comforting male superior and move into the climaxing female superior.

Side by Side — This position is favored by the Masters and Johnson Association because it provides equality for the man and woman. Each have the same amount of control for the rhythm and depth of penetration. It is also a user friendly position for the pregnant couple.

Hint: Because this position is rear entry, there is no physical contact to the clitoris. In order for her to achieve an orgasm in this position, you must also incorporate manual stimulation.

Doggy Style — This position enables you to achieve a deep level of penetration. Because of this, be aware that it could possibly be a painful experience for your partner. I recommend starting out slowly and asking her if it hurts, if not, penetrate a little deeper, ask again, etc.

Hint: Forget about any porno movies you have ever seen where the male slams and thrusts into a woman in this position. In reality that technique would be voted worst by most women.

As I have mentioned, there are many times during intercourse when manual stimulation is needed in order to provide an orgasm. The most effective and pleasurable way to administer manual stimulation is to use your whole hand and mimic the pressures which are achieved in the female dominant position. Remember not to use direct stimulation to the clitoris. Because it is such a sensitive area, direct contact can quickly become painful.

From these four basic positions, couples have created at least a hundred different techniques. Sitting, standing, hanging upside down — you name it, more than likely someone has tried it.

If you would like more information on different positions, Anne Hooper has many detailed books which provide illustrations and directions for numerous sexual positions. However, I honestly believe that your imagination can provide you with as many as you will ever need.

Experimenting with different sexual techniques can provide a relationship with variety and excitement. It can also be one of the best and most enjoyable learning experiences you will ever have.

I strongly suggest that every couple try at least one new technique a month and discover every possible pleasure.

● ● ●

BASIC SEXUAL TECHNIQUES

---

*"The source of sexual power is curiosity,
passion...sex does not thrive on monotony."*
—Anais Nin

Decisions, decisions... After deciding on what sexual position to use, you need technique. All of the following techniques add to the variety and different types of stimulation you can give and receive. One of the worst situations couples can fall into is repetition during sex: same way, same position, same technique. I am sure most men reading this have utilized all of these techniques at one time or another. This is just a reminder in case you have forgotten to use them lately.

Quickie — Done anywhere, anytime. Can be enjoyable and exciting, but should not be overused. Ideas for quickies include office lunch breaks, before work in the morning, unexpectedly pulling your car onto an abandoned parking lot... Let your imagination run wild!

Romantic — By far the favorite technique of women. Soft music, candles, fireplace, sensual talk. Use any position that enables you to look into her eyes — female superior, male superior, sitting face to face with her legs wrapped around you. Eye contact is extremely important. Foreplay and afterplay are a must.

Down and Dirty — The two words which describe this category are "passionate and aggressive." This is when you rip her clothes off (not literally in most cases) and make mad

89

passionate love to her. Pick any position — they will all work. Aggressive talk can add to the stimulation. Remember: passionate sex is not defined by throwing her up against a wall and banging her to death — this is not pleasurable for a woman. It does mean you can be slightly more aggressive with your rhythm and movements and still bring her pleasure.

Orgasmic Sex (For Her) — The most effective sexual technique for providing a woman with an orgasm is teasing. Teasing includes long foreplay — when reaching the point of the actual sex act, wait and go slow. Build as much anticipation as you possibly can without entering her. Tease her, but do not penetrate. Wait for her body movements or words to invite you in and then, even after that, go slow. When a woman is excited or aroused enough from teasing, she can have an orgasm almost instantly from the clitoral stimulation intercourse provides. Remember that intercourse by itself does not provide anticipation and, therefore, seldomly produces an orgasm.

Do not get caught up in all the different choices available for sexual positions and techniques. The most quality sex you can have is spontaneous and does not require a lot of thought. In order to make every sexual experience enjoyable, always appreciate the moment. Do not be preoccupied with the pursuit of either having or providing an orgasm. By doing this you are only concentrating on providing an ending and cannot fully appreciate the actual sex act. When couples get too hurried or concentrate on orgasm and don't take the time to feel what is happening to their bodies, they are not allowing themselves to enjoy the intense feelings and emotions that accompany the sex act.

Finally, I would like to discuss a falsehood I came across numerous times while researching information for this book. I found three books for men on a woman's sexuality, all of which were written by men, and all of which state that the most pleasurable time for a woman to have intercourse is right after she orgasms. If you've ever read this advice, forget it.

The first time I came across a book with this information I called many of my girlfriends to ask if it was a true statement, thinking that all women are not alike and that maybe another female could appreciate sex after orgasm. Not one person I asked enjoys sex after orgasm. To be very sure, I asked over 50 women, all of whom answered with a definite "no." They didn't even have to think it over.

This is the one thing most men and women have in common. Once they orgasm, they are done, maybe a little cuddling, then sleep. The only possible explanation I have for anyone who tells you different, is that more than likely the women they are describing didn't orgasm (faked it) and then yes, of course, they still want sex.

● ● ●

ORAL SEX

*"Graze on my lips; and if these hills be dry,
stray lower; where the pleasant fountains lie."*
—William Shakespeare

Not surprisingly, oral sex has been reported as "the preferred way to achieve orgasm" by many women. I am confident this reflects two ideas. One, some women have not yet learned to properly position themselves during intercourse and as a result cannot achieve orgasm by any means other than oral stimulation. And two, done right, it can be the most wonderfully sexual experience a woman can have.

Unfortunately, there are still some couples who consider this type of sexual technique taboo. As far as cunnilingus (oral sex performed on a woman) goes, there are many worries and inhibitions which interfere with enjoying this type of sexual gratification.

Women's inhibitions:

1. *They believe it is unsanitary.*
2. *They believe it is unnatural or weird.*
3. *They believe their natural odor may be offensive.*
4. *They believe they will not have a pleasant taste.*
5. *They worry that you will have a better view of their not-so-perfect body.*

Men's inhibitions:

1. *They believe it is unsanitary.*
2. *They believe it is unnatural or weird.*
3. *They worry that the natural odor will be offensive.*
4. *They worry that their partner will not have a pleasant taste.*
5. *They feel as if a real man should be able to satisfy his partner without all of the extras.*
6. *They fear they may not know how to satisfy their partner in this manner.*

If you notice, the inhibitions concerning oral sex between men and women are virtually the same. Let's go over them.

Unsanitary — The vagina, like the eye, is a self cleaning organ. Germ wise, it is cleaner than kissing a person. However, if this is a major worry to you or your partner, an easy solution is a long hot shower beforehand.

Unnatural or weird — This type of mentality reminds me of children talking about "Kooties." There is nothing unnatural or weird about oral sex. It is a perfectly normal way to enhance your sex life.

Natural odor — Many men find a woman's natural vaginal odor to be an extreme turn-on. If you do not fall into this category, again, a shower is recommended. If your partner still shows inhibitions, a douche can give her that cleaner than clean feeling.

Pleasant taste — For a little variety you can use chocolate syrup, honey, whipped cream, different flavored jellies, jams, etc.

Not-so-perfect-body — In this situation your partner needs verbal confirmation that her body is appealing to you.

A real man doesn't need the extras — This couldn't be further from the truth. There are many different ways to satisfy your partner and they all produce uniquely different sensations.

Being a quality sexual partner does not necessarily reflect your ability to have intercourse; it reflects your ability to be creative and satisfy your partner with as many pleasures as possible.

Fear of not being orally stimulating — We will cover this sexual technique in detail, however, as I have mentioned, different women have different desires and different triggers which stimulate them. For this reason, it is important to communicate and find out exactly what she likes or dislikes about oral sex.

When performing cunnilingus for the first time I highly recommend a hot shower or bath (which you can take together). This will help alleviate any worries about odor, taste, etc. Now for the details... Start out slowly, kissing and licking her whole body. Do not head straight for the pubic area. In general, the way a man performs oral sex will reveal how he will perform intercourse. You want to slowly and gradually taste her entire body. When approaching the pubic region tease her by kissing her inner thighs and all of the areas around her clitoris before actually stimulating her vaginal area. If you noticed, I have, and will, mention teasing often. Teasing builds anticipation and desire, both of which are necessary for quality sex.

As you start to pleasure her with your tongue, use general motions. By this, I do not mean concentrate your tongue pressure on any specific area. For example, some men use a sucking or pulling effect directly on a woman's clitoris. Done for a minute, this can be pleasurable. Done for longer it can be extremely painful. For maximum pleasure, use your entire mouth and generally stimulate the entire pubic region. Watch for her body signals, letting you know which techniques she likes best, or try experimenting with your tongue and softly ask her which one she likes best.

Another common mistake when performing oral sex is trying to use your tongue in place of a penis. When trying to push your tongue far up into a woman's vagina, you are not affecting the clitoris, therefore this technique does little for a woman's satisfaction, not to mention it can cause a great deal of strain on your tongue.

Here is a list of different ways to add variety to oral sex:

Use your hands — Remember when using your tongue, your hands are free to move around and caress her body, play with her nipples, etc. You can also use your fingers to stimulate the inside of her vagina or anus. Pick one or the other, because using the same finger from her anus to her vagina can be a health risk.

Vibrators — You can add extremely pleasant sensations when using a vibrator while performing oral sex.

Humming — Using your vocal cords to hum while performing oral sex can be as effective as a vibrator.

Tasty treats — As mentioned, you can incorporate a wide variety of foods and drinks into oral sex. This technique can be very helpful in using general stimulation. If you use a jelly or wine, more often you will lick the entire area in which it has been applied and are less likely to focus your attention on any one spot.

Sixty-nine — This position enables both of you to experience the pleasures of oral sex simultaneously. For those who have never tried this position it can be a wonderful experience. And for those who have, this is a reminder in case you have forgotten how exciting this position can be!

The most important thing to remember when performing cunnilingus is to be comfortable with her body and to make sure that she is also. When you verbally reaffirm how good she looks, how good she tastes, and how much you enjoy pleasuring her orally, you are helping to release any unnecessary inhibitions. The most common reason women do not enjoy receiving oral sex is because of worry and fear. Once you help her overcome these concerns she will feel free to relax and enjoy herself.

For the man who cannot get his partner to perform oral sex, her reasons are probably similar to the same reasons she may not want to receive it — worries and inhibitions. These two barricades can only be overcome with communication. As an example, I have a very close male friend who has been dating the same girl for close to a year. She very seldom performs oral sex, and when she does she is noticeably uncomfortable and awkward. This is a real problem with him and he expresses it to me frequently. However, he does not seem to like my answer: "Talk to her, show her what you like, let her know how important it is to you." To him, this advice is like telling a fat person to eat less and exercise — they don't want to accept the answer and are always looking for other solutions. I am no clairvoyant, but I can guarantee his situation will not change until he changes. The moral of this story is, do not let this be you! Talk, discuss and let her know how important oral sex is for your satisfaction. And when she does perform oral sex on you, tell her what you like and how you like it. Women, like men, are not mind readers. This is a situation where a little communication can go a long way.

Another suggestion that might be helpful is to take it slowly. There are many creative ideas throughout this book. Start by gradually using different techniques and after she experiences the multitude of pleasures she can give and receive, more than likely she will be more open to experimenting with oral sex.

On a final note, I would like to mention a small pet peeve of mine and a concern for many women I have talked with. There is nothing worse than a man who does not want to kiss after you have performed oral sex on him. This reminds me of the "kooties" thing again. It makes a woman feel like it is too "dirty" for your mouth, but it's O.K. for hers. Vaginal fluids and semen contain no harmful substances and the taste of both is extremely subtle. If using oral sex as foreplay, the mental interruption of "no kissing" can diminish a lot of pleasures during intercourse.

● ● ●

AFTERPLAY

"If you want to become a terrific lover, especially in showing your partner that you love her, then knowledge of afterplay is vital."
—Dr. Ruth

In the book *Afterplay: A Key to Intimacy*, Dr. Halpern and Dr. Sherman note, "What we found was that the success of a sexual relationship is more closely related to satisfaction with afterplay than with any other phase of the sexual encounter, foreplay, intercourse, even orgasm." What does this tell us? It tells us that the most frequently ignored phase of sexual encounters could very well be the most important.

Many men believe that afterplay is an emotional basic need for women. This is true, however, the physical changes a woman's body goes through after orgasm have just as much influence on her desire for afterplay. Let me explain: When a woman has an orgasm, her body slowly returns to her pre-excited condition. Because of this gradual return, her body is reversing through arousal states and therefore still feels the need for physical affection (A diagram of the physical process of a female orgasm is provided in Lesson 6: Multiple Orgasms). A man has the same physical changes, but much more rapidly. His physical changes can return to the pre-orgasmic state almost instantly. Thus, afterplay is commonly more important to women than men.

Well, now that you know that it is not only an emotional need but a physical need as well, it's time to talk about the "C" word — cuddle. I know you hate it, but it has to be said. I do not know if the word alone sounds too cutesy or feminine, but you don't often hear a man say he needs more cuddling. What I do know is that cuddling on occasion can do wonders for your relationship.

It may sound ridiculous, but believe me, the majority of women love, need and desire to be cuddled. It is hard to explain, but it is an emotional closeness that fulfills a woman's desire to be wanted, not just for sex, but also for love; it makes them feel warmth and compassion. So, even if you are not an avid cuddler, give it a try every now and then. The results you will see in your relationship will tell you more than I can about how important it is.

As with any part of your sexual relationship, variety is essential to afterplay. Take a shower or hot bath, or curl up and watch T.V. together. Discuss what part of your sexual experience was the best. There are many types of afterplay; use your imagination. If you are not up to talking or cuddling, and you just want to go to sleep, use the spoon position, wrap yourself around your partner, tell her how much you love her, and go to sleep — simple, effective afterplay.

One of my fondest memories of afterplay was with a man who would crawl out of bed after sex and play soothing music on the piano as I fell asleep. This might not seem like your typical afterplay, but that is the point. There are no specific rules to afterplay. The only general rule is to make your partner feel comfortable, wanted and loved.

Afterplay is not meant to be a burden and shouldn't feel like one. It should be considered part of the sex act, just the last part. It is a final confirmation of love, closeness and desire. Because afterplay is the last memory you have of your sexual encounter, it is important to make it a good one.

● ● ●

lesson

6

"The reason people sweat is so they don't catch fire when making love."
—Don Rose

In this lesson you will find many different varieties and techniques to intensify your sexual pleasure. Although all techniques may not be enjoyable for you, I highly recommend at least trying each once. You never know what you might discover. Using and trying different techniques can provide your sex life with unknown pleasures.

All of these suggestions will require a creative and open mind. These techniques are intended for couples who have overcome any and all of their inhibitions and are looking for ways to increase and enhance their sexual pleasures. As with any new technique, all of these should be discussed beforehand and desired by both individuals.

FANTASIES

***"The nice thing about fantasy is that it edits
out all of the bad parts."***
—Anthony Walsh

Although there are many differences between the male and female sexuality, fantasy is not one of them. Studies report that not only do men and women average the same amount of fantasies per day, but that the type of fantasies are almost identical (*New York Times, Sexual Fantasies: What are Their Hidden Meanings*, February 28, 1984). What are the most frequent fantasies?

For Men:
1. Replacement for established partner.
2. Forced sexual encounters with a woman.
3. Observing sexual activities.
4. Sexual encounters with men.
5. Group sex.

For Women:
1. Replacement for established partner.
2. Forced sexual encounters with a man.
3. Observing sexual activities.
4. Idyllic encounters with unknown men.
5. Sexual encounters with women.

As you will notice, the top three fantasies for both men and women are the same. The only difference is in how we fantasize. Typically, women are more detailed when imagining sexual experiences. They visualize more elaborate scenarios and often take longer to slowly work their way into a state of arousal. Men, on the other hand, tend to get straight to the point and reach arousal quickly, almost instantly.

Fantasies are completely normal and allow you to fulfill sexual desires you would never dream of doing in real life. For example, although forced sex is the second most used fantasy by women, in real life, rape is a woman's worst nightmare. Also, many people often fantasize about homosexual encounters while in reality they would be repulsed by the act. That is the whole idea of fantasy — not real.

There is no such thing as a wrong or bad fantasy. As I was growing into my own sexuality, I often thought my fantasies were weird or unnatural. It was not until I read the book *My Secret Garden,* by Nancy Friday, that my fears were put to rest. After reading this collection of other women's fantasies, I ended up feeling like June Cleaver. The moral of this story is that there seems to be no forbidden fruit when it comes to fantasy — everything and anything is normal.

Many couples enjoy acting out their sexual fantasies. This can be a very fun, playful and erotic experience. However, you do not want to be too specific when acting out fantasies or you might often be disappointed. In fantasyland you can provide yourself with an instant erection, you can shed twenty pounds off your partner, and every single act can go wonderfully smooth. In reality, this seldom happens.

To turn your fantasy into reality you need lenience. Start with a general idea, such as role playing doctor and patient, and let your real experiences come naturally. Have fun and play with new ideas and experiences. Let them evolve and unfold with spontaneity. Expecting real life to be identical to fantasy will only lead to frustration.

Another word of caution, there are some times when fantasies are better left untold. Often discussing fantasy can lead to hurt feelings and jealousy. If you fantasize about sleeping with her sister or best friend, or if your fantasy is something that may disturb her, it is better if you keep it to yourself. Also, be prepared. Usually when sharing your fantasies with your partner, she will in turn share her's. Make sure you are both mentally ready for this intimate discussion.

●　●　●

KINKY SEX

"Is sex dirty? Only if done right."
—Woody Allen

Kinky sex is an inhibited person's worse fear. I'm sure somewhere back in their minds are statements such as, "That's too weird for me," "It's disgusting," or "It's perverted." Even people who participate in kinky sex are often too embarrassed to admit it.

Before we go into the specifics of kinky sex, again let me clear the air. There is nothing abnormal or weird about having a multitude of sexual preferences. It is a healthy and normal way of sexual expression and can add great variety to couples who suffer from a humdrum sex life.

Just because I have categorized the techniques under the title "kinky" does not mean that they are not regularly practiced by many people. As a matter of fact, the large majority of couples have practiced at least one or more.

As with any sexual technique, it is important to make sure your partner is comfortable and willing to participate in these different activities. You should never pressure or force your partner into participating in any type of sexual activity. This will only cause stress and tension in a relationship.

Communicate your desires and preferences with your partner. Compromise and set limitations you are both comfortable with. You never know; through communicating with your partner, you might discover she has the same kinky desires, too.

If you don't experiment with different techniques, you might be missing out on one of the most pleasurable experiences of your life. If you find that you or your partner dislike a certain technique, try another until you have discovered all of your sexual pleasures. Remember that variety is the spice of life!

Anal Stimulation

If I said masturbation was a taboo subject, believe me, this one has it beat. Although studies have shown up to 35% of all couples have either tried or participate regularly in anal stimulation, it is still a technique few admit to utilizing.

There are three basic forms of anal stimulation: penetration, oral and manual.

Penetration — For the most part, anal sex is considered a "guy thing." I don't often hear of women complaining for lack of anal penetration. However, for some women, once they have tried it they find it to be exciting and pleasurable.

There are a few basic guidelines you should follow when participating in anal sex: 1) Cleanliness — Always wash the rectal area before penetration. A hot bath or shower is highly recommended. 2) Condom — Always use a condom to prevent infections. 3) Lubrication — Because the body doesn't produce natural lubricants for this area, artificial lubricants are necessary.

During penetration, "gentle" is not a strong enough word. For this situation, you need to take the word "gentle" and multiply it by one hundred. It is a good idea to start out slowly with a smaller object such as a lubricated dildo or your fingers. Gently loosen her rectal muscles and slowly insert your penis. Keep in mind this is completely different from entering the vagina; once you are inside of her you should not use powerful thrusts. The whole process from start to finish should be gentler and slower. It is extremely important for her to be relaxed and comfortable. If she is not mentally ready for anal sex, her rectal muscles will remain tight. This will cause a painful experience she will not readily want to reenact.

Oral — Because the rectal area is so sensitive, many couples have pleasurable experiences participating in oral stimulation. Again, cleanliness is next to godliness.

The most effective position for oral stimulation is to have your partner lie face down on the bed with a pillow tucked under her abdomen. This position enables you to reach her vagina and clitoris while orally stimulating her anus. The intensity can also be increased with the use of a vibrator.

Manual — As with penetration, it is important to use some type of lubrication to prevent discomfort. The most common technique for manual stimulation is to incorporate it with intercourse.

The most user-friendly positions are female superior and any position in which you are behind your partner. An example is doggy style. These positions provide you with the ability to gently probe her anus with your finger during intercourse.

Dirty Talk

You might be surprised to know that, according to *The Cosmo Report*, 49% of women surveyed report sexy talk as a turn-on. Dirty talk can be an erotic way to open up the lines of sexual communication. It can be an opportunity to tell your partner everything you sexually desire and vice versa.

If you are embarrassed starting a sexual conversation in person, take advantage of an opportunity when you are out of town. Call your partner and tell her everything you are going to do to her when you get home.

Be careful, too much assertiveness can have a negative effect. Some women are not only not turned-on by explicit terms, they can become offended. I suggest starting out slowly and finding a mutual comfort zone.

If you have never tried dirty talk and don't know where to start, here are some words that might help:

SOFT	**LICK**	**SWEATY**	**NECK**
HARD	**BITE**	**SLIPPERY**	**BUTT**
MOIST	**SUCK**	**TEASE**	**PROBE**
TENDER	**NIBBLE**	**STROKE**	**EXPLORE**
WET	**CARESS**	**NIPPLE**	**SEXY**
HARD	**HOT**	**BREAST**	**MOANING**
KISS	**STEAMY**	**THIGH**	**EXCITED**

If you noticed, none of the words used are pornographic. Using dirty talk does not necessarily mean you must use explicit words. However, if explicit dirty talk is what excites you, I am confident a few pornographic movies can provide you with a larger vocabulary.

Another good idea to help ease any discomfort is for you and your partner to call a 900 line, and listen together. This way neither of you has to do the talking, but can still find out which terms, phrases or words excite you.

Sneaky Sex

Adventurous or risky, whatever you call it, it is that adrenaline-inducing, excitement-building, almost-getting-caught sex.

I would imagine if you have experienced sex, at one time or another you have also experienced sneaky sex. Maybe you were at your parents' house or in the back seat at a drive in — anywhere that you had the slightest chance of getting caught.

If I asked you, "Describe the most exciting sex you have ever had," chances are good you would relate to sneaky sex of some sort. That is what exciting sex is all about — being exciting.

I am sure you have heard stories about "The Mile High Club" in which the only way to become a member is to have sex on an airplane. Or maybe you have heard stories of elevators, limousines, movie theaters, etc. Sneaky sex has added a spark to many couple's sexual experiences.

Unfortunately, sneaky sex is more likely to be used by either new relationships or younger couples. I have found that once couples are comfortable in a relationship they think they no longer need all of the whistles and bells. This is definitely not true. The most prevalent complaint by couples in a long-term relationship is lack of excitement. The most overlooked and obvious solution is simply to add some.

Obviously there are different levels of sneaky sex which vary from the slight possibility of getting caught (sex in the woods in the daytime), to a greater possibility (sex in a park in the

108

daytime). Make sure both you and your partner are comfortable with your "when and where" decisions.

Finally, I feel it is important to mention that whatever location and whatever risk is taken, both participants should be responsible enough to make sure there is absolutely no chance of being discovered by children. This is where fun and play can become unhealthy. Also, it is a good idea to minimize any chance of being caught by police, which could prove to be embarrassing and sometimes costly.

Sadomasochism

Unlike most sexual techniques, there are many forms of sadomasochism. There are a variety of accessories that include whips, chains, leather, leashes, etc. Techniques range from mild bondage to purposeful infliction of pain. Because of the large quantity of information in this category, I have decided to condense the information in this book to a milder form of sado-masochism: bondage. If you would like more information on this subject, I suggest reading the book *Kink,* by Susan Bakos.

Using bondage as a sexual technique requires a high level of trust and once again, both participants must be mentally prepared and willing. All limitations should be discussed and agreed upon before the actual encounter.

There are two roles when using bondage: the submissive and the dominant.

The Dominant — The dominant role has complete control. He/she is the person who does the tying. This role can be used to tease and stimulate your partner or can be used for your own sexual requests and satisfaction. Being in the dominant role, you decide what should be done and when.

The Submissive — The person in the submissive role is the one who is tied. He/she must participate in any actions the dominant requests. (Like you have a choice, you're tied up.) Note: Studies suggest that many women who normally experience inner guilt during sexual relations often feel freer to enjoy themselves while acting out a submissive role.

For your first encounter I would highly recommend using a very nonrestrictive form of bondage such as loosely tied silk scarves. This will enable both of you to get the general idea of bondage before going all out. Many times your partner may experience a high level of anxiety, fear, or a feeling of claustrophobia, during bondage. For this reason, many couples decide upon a safe word. This is a word that really means stop (many times during bondage, fantasy is also involved and the word "stop" does not necessarily mean stop). Your safe word will prevent any type of confusion.

Because bondage requires a high level of trust there are many people who are reluctant to try this technique. However, interestingly enough, people who have tried bondage report an *increased* level of trust and heightened sexual experiences.

● ● ●

SEX GAMES

***"Sex play, like foreplay is the icing
on the carnal cake....."***
—Sex Secrets

A quality sex life contains many different facets. There are times it should be romantic, times it should be sensual, times it should be downright dirty and times it should be just plain ol' fun. If you are the kind of person who takes your sex life too seriously, this lesson is for you.

Variety is key in adding excitement to your relationship. In a quality sexual relationship there is no embarrassment or shyness. There should be a freedom shared between both partners allowing for the serious and silly.

For many people, their most creative sex was when they where first beginning to experience sex. I wonder why that is? Maybe because you are less inhibited at a young age? Or maybe more inquisitive about sex? Whatever the reason, I find this holds true for many people. It seems everyone grows up into mature individuals who worry about work and money and forget the basic enjoyments of life.

It is time to get back to the basics and stop taking sex so seriously. At times sex needs to be fun and playful. It helps to break down walls of inhibitions and adds a special twist to taking the stress out of the day.

When was the last time you laughed and played while having sex? There are so many times that you need to be a dad, a boss or an employee. When was the last time you were just a kid having some fun? For the sanity of the world, I think everyone needs to play a little more, and what better place to play than in the bedroom.

Keep in mind, when playing sex games, your goal is not to give your partner an orgasm; it is to have fun and maybe learn a little in the process. While playing sex games, do not worry about techniques or performance. Sex games are for nothing other than mischievous fun and a renewal of inner youth.

THE COOKIE JAR

Number of players: *2*

Supplies needed: *1 pair of scissors and a cookie jar*

Assembly: *Cut out each of the activity slips, fold in half, place in cookie jar*

Game summary: *When you feel your sex life needs a little spicing up, you or your partner can pick one activity slip from the cookie jar (no peeking). There are 52 activity slips to pick from — one for every week in the year. This is a great way to add instant variety and can also be a good way to break the ice after an argument. You can pick from your cookie jar as often or as little as needed.*

Optional Play: *To add excitement to all 52 weeks of the year, you can choose one specific day to pick an activity slip and then choose another to accomplish it.* **Example:** *Every Monday morning pick a slip, with a one-week goal to accomplish the activity. This will give you something to think about and look forward to all week. One word: Anticipation.*

Rules: *Only one activity slip can be picked per session. You cannot keep picking to find your favorite slip! Save each activity slip in a separate container to be reused when cookie jar is empty.*

Object of game: *To add a little excitement and playfulness to your day.*

DIRTY DANCING

Give him a strip show.

TAKE IT OFF

Give her a strip show.

A TOUCH OF CLASS

Check into a nice hotel for a romantic night for two.

NO TELL-MOTEL

Check into a cheesy hotel that rents by the hour.

EVE'S DELIGHT

Give her a thirty minute massage.

ADAM'S DELIGHT
Give him a 30 minute massage.

SUNDAE DELIGHT
Add a little chocolate sauce and whipped
cream to tonight's agenda.

DREAM LOVER
Act out his favorite fantasy.

LET'S PRETEND
Act out her favorite fantasy.

BLIND DATE
Blindfold him for a night of passion.

NO PEEK
Blindfold her for a night of passion.

10-W DIRTY
Get out the baby oil and have some fun!

RED HOT!
Have sex in front of a fireplace...don't have one?
Even more fun, find one.

RISKY BUSINESS
There are two rules for your next sexual encounter.
One, don't get caught. Two, pick a place where you might.

RUB A DUB DUB
Give him a hot bubble bath, wash him and dry him off.

SPLISH SPLASH

Give her a hot bubble bath, wash her and dry her off.

SLIPPERY WHEN WET

Take a shower together.

NATURE LOVER

Have sex anywhere outdoors.

INTIMATE APPAREL

Dress up in sexy lingerie for him.

SORRY CHARLIE

No sex tonight. Cuddle, cuddle, cuddle.

LUNCH BREAK
Meet your partner for an afternoon quickie.

COPY CAT
Rent a dirty movie and mimic their moves.

CANDID CAMERA
Get out your camcorder and make your own dirty movie.

GENIE
Grant one sexual wish for him.

ALADDIN
Grant one sexual wish for her.

PASSION PREMIER
Try something you have never tried before.
Use some imagination!

STEAMY SENSATIONS
Have sex in a whirlpool or hot tub.

MIDNIGHT SNACK
Wake him up for some late-nite fun.

TIGHT SQUEEZE
Pretend you're on a date and have sex in your car.

EXCITING FORECAST
Save this for the next rainy day. Make love in the rain.
For now, pick again.

BEDTIME STORIES
Read erotic stories to each other.

THE MAID
Be his sexual slave for the night.

THE BUTLER
Be her sexual slave for the night.

SEXY NIGHT
Masturbate in front of him tonight.

TANTALIZING TURN-ON
Masturbate in front of her tonight.

HIS WINNING TICKET

Satisfy him orally for as long as he wants.

HER WINNING TICKET

Satisfy her orally for as long as she wants.

WILD CARDS

Play a game of strip poker.

WET AND WILD

Find a lake, ocean or pool and go skinny dipping.

NOW YOU'RE COOKING!

Make love on the kitchen counter.

GOOD VIBRATIONS
Have sex on the spin cycle.

LOOK-OUT POINT
Have sex anywhere that has a great view.
Ideas: On a mountain top, the top floor of a hotel,
the ocean at dawn. . . Be creative!

PERFECT PURCHASE
Go together to a sex store, buy a new toy and try it out!

LIGHT YOUR FIRE
Light up your bedroom with candles.

THE PERFECT HOSTESS
Serve him dinner in the nude.

MOVING VIOLATION
Find an elevator. . .

THE ROMANTIC
Have romantic, soft, sensual sex and then
fall asleep in each other's arms.

DOUBLE PLEASURE/DOUBLE DELIGHT
Enjoy your sexual encounter in front of the
biggest mirror in the house.

The last four activity strips (following page) were left blank so that you and your partner can fill in your own creative pastime. You may repeat a favorite activity or add your own technique!

HIS ACTIVITY

HER ACTIVITY

HIS ACTIVITY

HER ACTIVITY

WHEEL OF WISHES

Number of players: *2*

Supplies needed: *Scissors and a creative imagination*

Game summary: *Each wheel contains six empty sections which represent six nights of the year. These nights should be considered "His Night" or "Her Night." When redeeming a night, you are entitled to all of the sexual attention and pampering, without an obligation to please your partner. These are truly wishful nights. With these nights you are also granted three wishes from your partner.* **Example of play:** *You have a hard day at work, you are tired and would like an evening of your own. You redeem a night on your wheel and ask for three wishes: 1) your partner serves you dinner in sexy lingerie; 2) after dinner she gives you a massage; and 3) she pleases you with oral sex before you go to sleep (I bet you like this game already). The catch here is that your partner can also redeem her wheel at a time of her choosing and you will be required to give her a night of three wishes without satisfying any of your own.*

Rules: *Once you have received your night, you must mark off a space on your wheel. There are three spaces marked "unexpected." These spaces can be used without advanced notice, anytime, day or night. For consideration, the other spaces should only be redeemed after a minimum of 24 hours notice, in case the wish granter has had a long, hard day also, and doesn't want to be surprised with a night of giving. Since your main goal* *throughout the year should be based on the mutual pleasure you both receive from satisfying each other, there are only six nights available per person. Because, however enjoyable they may be, they are also extremely self-indulgent.*

Object of Game: *Everyone needs to have a special night every once in a while to feel pampered and important without obligation to reciprocate. This gives both you and your partner the opportunity to completely focus on your own fulfillment. This is the time everyone needs to just sit back, relax and enjoy.*

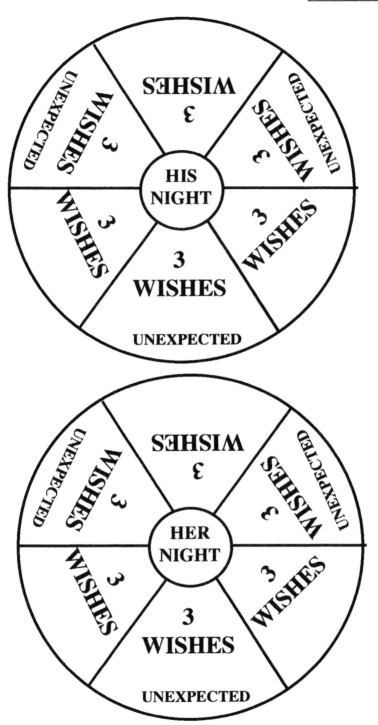

BODY BINGO

Number of players: *2*

Supplies needed: *Red-hots or chocolate kisses, and a blindfold. Before you start: Both players must be extremely clean; a hot shower beforehand is recommended.*

Game summary: *One player is selected to go first. The first player picks out five spots on his/her body and marks them with either a wet red hot (the coloring of the red hot serves as a marker) or a warmed chocolate kiss, marking different spots with the soft chocolate. The second player is blindfolded and sent on a mission to orally find the marked spots. When the first marked spot is found, player one must announce a "B." For the second, "I." For the third, "N." For the fourth, "G." When the last spot is found, "Bingo." When player two reaches "Bingo," he/she has officially won the game. The player roles are now switched.*

Rules: *Hands do not count. If a player touches the marked spot with anything other than the tongue he does not get a letter. Once you begin searching for a spot, your partner can wait no more than two minutes to announce a letter or you must move to a different location on the body and try again. There is no time limit on this, the game is not over until all spots are found. Be creative and imaginative when marking different spots. After all, the harder they are to find, the longer it will take to find them — that's why this game is so fun! Examples: Back of neck, eyelid, between toes, pinkie finger, etc.*

Object of Game: *To explore every inch of your partner's body and find new highly erotic areas.*

You can also find a wide variety of games in adult stores. Some of the more popular games are:

Strip Poker — Most adult stores carry a modified card deck for strip poker.

Dirty Dice — Custom designed dice with body parts on one die — neck, breast, lips, etc., and actions — bite, lick, and suck, etc., — on the other. Roll the dice and have some fun!

Between the Sheets — An exciting sexual version of twister.

Strip Checkers — Game pieces are marked so that with each piece captured you have to remove an article of clothing.

For Lovers Only — An erotic board game.

Dirty Pictures — A sexual version of pictionary.

Adult games allow you to have pressure-free sex. The purpose of these games is not necessarily to achieve orgasm but, more importantly, to explore and discover each other's sexuality. For any man who suffers from performance anxiety, this can be quite helpful. Contrary to popular belief, it is O.K. to mess up, fumble and laugh during sex. It can make for extremely memorable sex and also bring a friendship and closeness to your sex life. There are many times it is important to incorporate fun and laughter into your sexual experiences.

Adult games also help reduce sexual inhibitions. If there are no fears of sexual performance you are more likely to open yourself up to new experiences. There is a lot to be said for silly and fun sexual bonding. By exposing your inner child you can bring a closeness into your relationship that cannot be found through any other sexual techniques.

So let loose with your partner and have some fun! Learn and grow with each other. Don't be afraid of making mistakes, mistakes are nothing more than a lesson. Hopefully, during the course of your relationship you will have many different types of sex. But, some of the best sex you will ever have is the playful sex that when you think about the next day, makes you laugh out loud. That's when you can truly say you have an uninhibited sexual relationship.

● ● ●

MULTIPLE ORGASM

"Love's climax should never be rushed, I say, but worked up slowly, lingering all the way."
—Ovid

According to *The Cosmo Report,* 76% of women surveyed have had multiple orgasms on occasion and 10% always have them. According to my math, that leaves 24% who have never had the pleasure of experiencing multiple orgasms. Because almost all women are physically capable of achieving multiple orgasms, I believe knowledge is the key for those missing out.

The art of providing your partner with multiple orgasms is easier, if first you are familiar with the anatomy of an orgasm. There are four basic stages to an orgasm: the initial excitement, the building of excitement, the orgasmic phase and the resolution. During all of these stages her body has significant physical changes (blood pressure, flushed skin, etc.).

During the initial excitement and the building of excitement, the sexual adrenaline increases. The orgasmic phase is the release of this adrenaline and during the resolution phase her body slowly returns to the pre-excitement state.

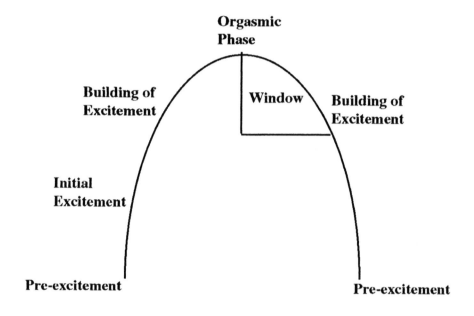

During the slow regression of the resolution stage, the physical changes that have occurred during the achievement of orgasm are repeated as they return to the pre-excitement stage. This is her window for multiple orgasms, because her body is going through the exact same changes after an orgasm. As she physically declines to the building of excitement phase, she has the ability to orgasm again, and after that orgasm, as she is declining, once again, etc. Hence, multiple orgasms.

Although there is a window of time available for multiple orgasms, it is a very small window. The time period to attain multiple orgasms can be less than five minutes. In other words, if your goal is to give your partner multiple orgasms, there cannot be an intermission after the first orgasm. In order to achieve multiple orgasms, you must maintain contact with the clitoris after her initial orgasm.

Because a woman's clitoris can be extremely sensitive after orgasm, the degree of direct contact should be minimal. After her initial orgasm, apply general stimulation to her entire pubic area. It is extremely important to remember the words "general stimulation."

Multiple orgasms can be a wonderful experience for a woman — they have been described as "a thousand times better than a regular orgasm." Your ability to provide your partner with this type of experience can enhance your sexual encounters immensely. When a woman, or anyone for that matter, is overwhelmed with physical pleasure they tend to try and give the same amount of pleasure in return. This is what makes quality sex.

Experiment and be creative. Multiple orgasms can be achieved manually, orally or with intercourse. Since all women have different intensities of orgasms, find out what techniques pleasure your partner the most. And, if first you don't succeed, try, try again. Practicing sexual methods is one of the few things in life in which you can enjoy the work as much as the reward.

lesson 7

"The source of sexual power is curiosity, passion...
Sex does not thrive on monotony."
—Anais Nin

There will be times in everyone's life when adjustments in their sexual practices are needed. This lesson will help prepare you for these situations.

Always remember: There should never be a time in your sex life when sex isn't extremely pleasurable and exciting.

Any obstacles which may affect your sex can be easily cured with small modifications. Once the changes have been made, your sexual experiences can be as good, if not better, than they ever were.

FIRST TIME SEX

"...the major factor in whether a first sexual encounter is pleasant or distressing seems to be the same factor that always affects the pleasurableness of sex: the quality of the relationship between the lovers."
—Linda Wolff, *The Cosmo Report*

Whether it is the first time a woman has ever had sex or the first time she is having sex with you, it can be an uncomfortable, maybe even awkward situation. Let's first talk about having sex with a partner who is a virgin. Although you have the ability to give your partner a truly wonderful experience, it will be extremely difficult and almost impossible to bring her to orgasm. *The Cosmo Report* interviewed 106,000 women and of those, 95 percent did not have an orgasm the first time and I believe the five percent left might have been stretching the truth a little.

The first time a woman has sex there are a multitude of mental obstacles to overcome in order to achieve orgasm. She not only has the self esteem questions to deal with — "Does he find me attractive?" "Does he respect me?" — but also — "Is this the right time?" "Should I be doing this?" "Is this all he wanted?" "Now that he's got it, will I lose him?" "Does he love me?" "Am I doing this right?" "Is it going to hurt?" There is too much internal dialogue occuring for a woman to concentrate on having an orgasm. She doesn't know exactly what to expect and there is a certain fear of the unknown.

Consider anything else that was exciting the first time you tried it: riding a bike or motorcycle, or learning to skate. It is an enjoyable experience, but are you really concentrating on enjoying your experience? When learning anything new, the first time you are concentrating on learning, not failing, doing it right, worrying that you're not doing it right, being nervous and hoping that you'll master the situation. Get my point?

Remember that her first sexual encounter can affect the way she feels about sex throughout her lifetime. Always go slowly! Make it as pleasurable as it can be and try to remove any distractions before they surface. Make sure her mind is at ease, let her know you respect her, compliment her body. This will help to make her first learning experience an enjoyable one. Help her to explore her body, find out what she enjoys and what pleasures her. After all, if she has never had sex before, she doesn't even know what it is supposed to feel like.

During her first sexual encounter, a generous amount of foreplay is crucial. When a female is nervous, her body does not secrete the vaginal fluids necessary for comfortable sex. With increasing the amount of foreplay you can change an otherwise painful experience into a pleasurable one.

This will be the only time throughout this book that I will tell you to give up on the expectation of giving your partner an orgasm — your odds are slim at best. Just be patient, gentle and understanding, and you can change what most women feel is a painful or disagreeable experience, into a wonderfully pleasant memory. With that you will have accomplished more than most men.

If your partner has experienced sex before but it is the first time experiencing it with you, it can also prove to be an awkward situation. She may wonder if she is as good as your previous partners and feel intimidated about her sexual performance. There is also a fear of having too much sexual knowledge, and that you might think she is cheap or easy. Whatever her thought process, there are many mental distractions that can interfere with her sexual pleasure.

When having relations with a partner for the first time, your most important mission is to make sure she is at ease and comfortable. First time sex should be for learning and exploring and should be slow and sensual. This is not the right time to show her the 32 positions you have mastered. First time sex can be awkward in itself without putting unnecessary pressures on you or your partner. Save the acrobatic sessions for future encounters.

Most importantly, do not pressure your partner into having sex. Regardless if she has experienced sex before, for her to enjoy her first sexual experience with you, she has to be mentally and emotionally ready. This is the time you need to practice patience. For this lesson the key words to remember are: gentleness, patience and understanding. These three words put into action can provide a pleasurable experience.

● ● ●

SEX AND PREGNANCY

*"There is not a more beautiful sight
than a woman with child."*
—Jim Lapides

A common question asked by many pregnant couples is, "Is it safe to have sex and if so, at what point in the pregnancy should we stop?" Unless you have been restricted by a physician you can have sex as often as you would like up until the time of labor.

As a matter of fact, many women report an increased sex drive during pregnancy. This is in part due to the increased hormonal activity affecting her body. Although she may be experiencing an unusually high libido, safety precautions need to be taken to ensure safe, pleasurable sex.

The safest and most effective positions are: side by side, female dominant and rear entry. You should not continue using the missionary position after the fourth month of pregnancy. Certain blood vessels can be cut off when she is lying on her back for long time periods and the added weight of a man on top can only worsen the situation.

During pregnancy it is also important to use minimal stimulation on her nipples. When overly stimulated, her nipples can release a hormone that can cause painful uterine contractions. Also, during the course of her pregnancy, her nipples can become swollen and tender, making them painful to the touch. This is a great opportunity to find out what other areas of her body are erogenous.

The psychological effects of pregnancy can be damaging to your sexual relationship. Your partner may feel fat and unappealing. She may compare herself to other women and feel that she is not as attractive.

It is important that you help her overcome these negative feelings. You can help put her mind at ease by continually communicating her beauty. When a woman is pregnant there is no such thing as giving too many compliments. She needs all of your support and affection during these uncomfortable months.

Done correctly, sex during pregnancy can be a unique bonding experience for both partners. Take advantage of this time to bring closeness and love into your sexual relationship.

● ● ●

SEX AND THE SENIOR

"May your fire never go out."
—Traditional Irish Toast

Unfortunately, the influence Father Time has on our sexuality can be less than kind. The physical changes that occur can affect both partners physically and physiologically. However, it is important to remember that although there are small adjustments needed to accommodate the sexual aging process, it can be as pleasurable and exciting as ever.

Women

As a woman ages, her vagina becomes drier and her ability to produce vaginal fluid decreases. A common misconception is that this stems from lack of desire. On the contrary, the decrease of vaginal fluid is only a natural physical occurrence and is not a sign of a low libido.

This problem easily can be solved with over-the-counter lubricants. It is important to use these lubricants when needed. Dry sexual intercourse can be an uncomfortable experience and with lack of pleasure you can very possibly create a lack of sex drive.

There are also many psychological barriers women can build. They may be embarrassed from the effects aging has had on their body and become more inhibited. She may think she is *too old* for sex. If you are having problems with achieving an erection, she will often put the blame on herself and mentally confirm her unattractiveness.

The psychological effects of aging can be much more damaging than the physical. Most sexual problems due to aging can be quickly fixed. However, psychological problems require patience and communication, and can take a lot longer to overcome.

Men

As a man ages his testosterone level decreases, but this does not necessarily mean his sex drive decreases along with it. It simply means that more time and stimulation is needed to produce an orgasm.

There is actually a plus side to this situation. If a variety of stimulation is needed, your partner will have to provide a little more creativity to your sexual encounters. This is a perfect time to experiment with new ideas and techniques to enhance your sexual encounters.

Aging can also produce the more serious problem of impotence. Impotence can often be a side effect of medication or another medical problem. Before worry starts to set in, speak with a physician. Many times a simple change in medication can solve the problem.

If there is no medical condition found, you might be experiencing short-term impotence. This is a type of anticipatory anxiety that can very often affect the ability to attain or sustain erection. In this case, the fear of not being able to achieve erection is what prohibits the actual erection.

Again, do not worry. Short-term impotence is just that — short-term. It can be overcome easily with a patient and understanding partner. You should mentally set aside the need for an erection and continue satisfying your partner manually or orally. Once again, you should get creative and experiment with different sexual and masturbation techniques. Any problems of short-term impotency will disappear the moment you realize you can achieve an erection and stop worrying about being able to achieve another one.

And, so what if you have discovered your short-term impotency is not exactly short-term. There are still resources available that can enable you to have a quality sex life, including a variety of implant devices that can give you the opportunity to achieve erection whenever you want. There are also many vitamins available which can help alleviate most symptoms. And the new drug Viagra has finally been released and has proven results in over 90% of users.

If you are suffering from any type of impotency, it is important for you to share this with your partner and doctor. These are the two people who can help you emotionally and physically.

Since many men are embarrassed confronting this problem, you should know, it is plain ridiculous to be embarrassed by impotency. It is a natural, normal physical change that affects thousands of men. Any other problem that occurs during later years such as arthritis, gray hair or loss of vision can be discussed without the slightest bit of embarrassment, but since the penis is directly connected to the male ego, a man can barely utter the word impotence. For your sake and for your partner's, you need to communicate any problem you may be having. This is a problem that has a solution, but until it is discussed with a physician, it will remain a problem.

As I have mentioned, there are small adjustments needed to accommodate mature sex, but they are not necessarily all negative. Here are a few of the more positive adjustments to look forward to:

Children —*There are no longer children knocking on the door asking what you are doing, or unexpected walk-ins. You now* have the freedom to have sex on the kitchen table, in the middle of the afternoon, if you'd like. For many people this is the first time they can truly experience uninhibited sexual relations.

Fertility — There are no underlying worries of pregnancy that may have interfered with your sexual satisfaction. Assuming you are in a monogamous relationship, there are no pills, condoms or diaphragms to interfere with foreplay. If in the past you have used the withdrawal method for birth control, sex without withdrawal can create an entirely new experience.

Time — No matter how enjoyable your sex life is, after a long day at work your energy level and your sex drive can be depleted. If you have reached retirement, you now have the time you spent at work for enjoying the more pleasurable things in life.

Creativity — Many times couples who have never been creative before find it necessary in the golden years. This can often provide sensually gratifying experiences they have never known before.

As you can see, there are many enjoyments that accompany mature sex. Having a quality sexual life can help keep the spark in a relationship. Now that you actually have the time to enjoy sex, whatever you do, don't give it up now.

lesson

8

A QUESTIONNAIRE FOR YOUR PARTNER

"Knowledge itself is power."
—Francis Bacon

Throughout this book I have stressed how extremely important it is to have open communication about sex with your partner. It is essential in discovering what pleases and displeases her. It gives you the limitations to what she feels comfortable with, and aids in turning your relationship into an open, honest friendship. If you can learn to freely discuss your sexual desires, you will naturally be more comfortable with any other discussion that might come up.

Ideally, this questionniare should be given as an oral exam, however, for the couples who are still not comfortable discussing sex, I have designed it so that you can each fill it out separately. Hopefully, when she fills it out and gives it back to you, her answers will spark a conversation.

155

The following questionnaire is almost identical to the one given to the clients in my salon, when I was acquiring information for this book. Each person who received a questionnaire was told that it would be held in strictest confidence. My only requirement was that all answers would be blatantly honest. Although many of the answers were alike, each had their own individuality. For example, there were many women who complained about lack of romance, but each woman's definition of romance was slightly different.

Every woman has her own specific ideas that spark her passion. In each lesson I have given you the basics as to how a woman thinks, feels and what she desires. The answers you receive with this questionnaire will enable you to discover the finer details.

Most importantly, this questionnaire should be filled out without fear of repercussions. The intended goal of this questionnaire is to increase your partner's pleasure; there is no room for criticism or jealousies. Because this might be the first honest information you have had about her sexual preferences, you could have some startling answers. Remember, there are no right or wrong answers There should be no judgments made. There are certain questions that may instinctively make you want to react in a critical way. For example, question #18 asks you to think back to your best sexual encounter. What made it so good? What if the answer to that question is a sexual encounter your partner has had with someone else? This is what you need to think about before giving this to your partner. Make sure you are ready for the answers no matter what they are.

Do not take any comments your partner makes as an insult. Take each question for what it is, confident information your partner is sharing with you. This is the stuff she shares with her girlfriends; these are her innermost feelings. You would not be able to grow in your sexual relationship if your partner answered every question the way she thought you wanted her to answer it.

If there is an answer that you don't feel comfortable with, great! That means there's room for more discussion. I want you to talk and discuss your sex life so much that you know as much about her desires as she does. This knowledge is what will enable you to make any changes necessary to increase her sexual satisfaction.

It is just as important for her to know what pleasures you. For mutual satisfaction you should also discuss your answers or duplicate this questionnaire and give the completed pages to your partner.

QUESTIONNAIRE

This questionnaire has been designed to improve the quality of your sex life as well as the quality of your relationship. Please be completely honest with your answers. Feel free to write on a separate piece of paper if additional space is needed.

1) I would like to have sexual relations:
A) more frequently B) less frequently C) about the same

2) At what time of the day do you prefer to make love?
A) morning B) during the day C) at night

Why?_____

_____

_____

_____

3) What is your favorite love-making position?

_____

Why?_____

_____

_____

_____

4) Have you ever faked orgasm?
A) yes B) no

If yes, when and why?

_____

_____

_____

5) Since your first sexual experience, how often have you faked an orgasm?
A) always B) most of the time C) occasionally D) rarely E) never

6) Have you ever had a sexual experience that was completely dissatisfying?
a) yes B) no

If yes, why was it dissatisfying?

_____

_____

_____

_____

_____

7) How important is foreplay to you?

_____

8) How long do you usually like foreplay to last?

_____

_____

9) What do you like best about foreplay?

_____

_____

_____

10) Would you consider yourself inhibited about any of the following?
A) weight B) sexual skills C) body shape
D) other_____

11) If you do have inhibitions, how often do they interfere with your sex life?
A) always B) sometimes C) rarely D) never

12) Is your current sex life satisfactory?
A) yes B) no

If no, what could be done to improve your current sexual relations?

_____

_____

_____

13) What is your favorite setting to make love, aside from the bedroom?
Examples: floor, tub, outdoors, car, shower, etc.

_____

_____

_____

14) What type of ambiance do you like when making love? Examples: candles, music, etc.

_____

_____

_____

15) How important is oral sex to you?
A) extremely B) somewhat C) not important at all

16) How do you prefer to achieve orgasm?
A) oral sex B) hand manipulation C) male dominant
D) female dominant E) Other_____

17) Think back to your best sexual encounter. What made it so good?

_____

_____

_____

18) Have you ever had multiple orgasms?
A) yes B) no

19) Do you experience any pain or discomfort during intercourse?
A) yes B) no

20) Are you inhibited about trying new sexual experiences?
A) yes B) no

If yes, what are your inhibitions?

_____

_____

_____

21) Do you believe your sexual satisfaction is important to your partner?
A) yes B) no

22) Do you believe your sex drive is more mental, physical or emotional?

_____

_____

23) Do you believe your partner's sex drive is more mental, physical or emotional?

_____

24) Does communication play a large role in your sex life?

_____

25) How important is afterplay?
A) extremely B) somewhat C) not important at all

Why or why not?

_____

_____

_____

26) Do your orgasms vary in intensity?
A) often B) sometimes C) never

If you answered often or sometimes, what do you believe makes them more intense?

_____

_____

_____

27) How often do you masturbate?
A) every day B) several times a week C) several times a month
D) rarely E) never

28) What means do you use to masturbate?
A) hand B) vibrator C) dildo D) water pressure
E) other_____

29) Do you currently own a vibrator or dildo?
A) yes B) no

30) Do you enjoy participating in any fetishes?
A) bondage B) sadomasochism C) voyeurism
D) other_____

31) Is there a particular fetish you have not tried but have fantasized about?

_____

_____

_____

32) Do you believe your partner would change his sexual habits in order to improve your sex life?
A) yes B) no

33) How important is romance in your sexual relationship?

_____

_____

_____

34) Name three of your favorite romantic gestures.

_____

_____

_____

35) Please list five suggestions your partner could use to improve the quality of your sex life.

_____

_____

_____

_____

_____

36) Is there anything that you would never consider doing?

_____

_____

CONCLUSION

"Do I really have to do all of this stuff?"
—Andy Bordeman
(a friend, after reading the first copy of this book)

When I first started writing the foreword to this book I used the analogy of an orchestra to portray the importance of each specific lesson. At the time, I thought it was an adequate analogy and a good way to get my point across. I have to admit that even while writing it, I did not fully realize how important it was.

As I wrote, I found myself wanting to preface every single lesson with, "This is the most important lesson to learn." Then I would get to the next lesson and think to myself, "No, this is the most important information they need to know." It was never ending; every lesson is "the most important."

You have to understand that while putting this together, I used the information from women who have patronized my beauty salon for years and also knowledge from my own personal experiences. There was not one lesson that I didn't personally relate to in one way or another and I am sure that is why I felt so emphatic about each lesson.

Somewhere along the line I realized that the orchestra analogy was not just a good analogy, but a great one — that there is no technique that takes precedence over the others and that they are all necessary. And that, I can honestly say is the most important lesson. It took writing this book to truly understand this concept and I can only hope that while reading you began to learn as I did.

I also have to admit that I did not realize the true complexity of a woman. Being a woman I have the upper hand on what is satisfying to me and talking with other women only confirmed in my mind that our needs were simple. I knew that many men did not understand what was needed to sexually satisfy their partner, but I didn't understand why. After all, I am a woman and I understand completely.

I honestly thought that this publication would be half the size. As I wrote I received input from every one of my female friends who would tell me, "Don't forget about this," and "Don't forget to mention that." Or, I would come across something in an article or a book, and would think to myself, "I can't believe I almost forgot to put that in, it is essential."

After adding all the bits and pieces, and essentials, I became aware that satisfying a woman is not as easy as I had originally thought. Once I had written it all down in black and white, instead of just feeling it, I was surprised to see how much information was actually needed. Now, I finally understand why men have always said that women are a confusing bunch.

Even though a woman's needs can seem overwhelming or

maybe even impossible to fill, by starting out slowly with one or two lessons a month, I am sure you will quickly notice improvements in your own satisfaction and look forward to trying additional lessons. It is kind of like this wonderful sensual snowball effect. You try a lesson, you see results, you try another, you see even more results. The next thing you know you are involved in the best sexual relationship you have ever had.

Just by purchasing and reading this book you have proven you have the desire to improve your partner's sexual satisfaction. That in itself is 50 percent of the battle. As you have read, building a quality sexual relationship takes effort and initiative, but I am confident your effort will be rewarded. I wouldn't be surprised if your partner didn't begin to initiate sex more, and maybe even become a little more creative and experimental when pleasuring you.

Therapists used to believe that a quality relationship was needed to provide quality sex. They are just starting to experiment with the idea that quality sex can provide for a quality relationship. I tend to like this theory. If you think about it, aren't you more likely to want to share your days with someone who makes your nights extremely pleasurable? I truly believe that, when making improvements to your sexual relationship, every aspect of your relationship will benefit.

Finally, I would like to share with you the most recent lesson I have learned on the importance of a quality sexual relationship. I met a woman who is in her second marriage and she told me how wonderful it is in comparison to her first. One of the first things she mentioned is that her sexual life is much more satisfying. After talking with her further, I told her that I was just completing a book on sexually satisfying a woman. After making the comment that she should buy a copy and send it anonymously to her ex-husband, she started expressing how important she thought this type of book was, and how crucial sex was in her relationship. I was not surprised by her comments, because this is the typical response I received from most women. Then she told me something I hadn't heard before. She said that her satisfying sex life has had a wonderful impact on her children.

I had no clue of what she was talking about and had to question her further. She said that for the first time in her life she has a quality sexual relationship. She has found somebody who experiences pleasure in pleasuring her and in turn she feels the same. Her satisfaction in her sex life and her freedom to express herself has given her a new outlook on relationships. She loves her husband and has never been happier in her life. She told me that she is extremely pleased to finally be able to provide her children with an example of a quality relationship. And, she believes living in an environment where there is an abundance of love makes them healthier and happier. She hopes that after seeing what a relationship should be, they will expect and aspire to bring the same happiness into their future relationships.

This conversation made a big impact on me because I had never considered the possibility that the benefits of quality sex would affect more than the two partners involved. I quickly realized that her quality sex life had not only affected her children, but it had also affected me. And, I am sure it has touched many other people who have seen the twinkle in her eye and wished themselves that lucky.

The truth is, with a little initiative and understanding, anyone can bring the same joy into their own relationships. I believe that one of the greatest gifts God has given us is being able to achieve physical pleasure and closeness through intimacy. It is free, it is enjoyable, it helps bond relationships, and all in all, I can't think of a better pastime! Good Luck.

Sharon Colona

P.S. — I love to hear success stories. If you have a story you would like to share or have any questions or comments about the lessons, please write to:

Sharon Colona
c/o Frederick Fell Publishers, Inc.
2131 Hollywood Blvd.
Hollywood, FL 33020

REFERENCES

Bakos, Susan. *Kink.* New York: TOR Books, 1995.

Chichester, Brian, Robinson, Kenton, and the Editors of Men's Health Books. *Sex Secrets.* Emmaus, Pennsylvania: Rodale Press, Inc., 1996.

Friday, Nancy. *My Secret Garden.* New York: Pocket Books, 1973.

Godek, Gregory J.P. *1001 Ways to be Romantic.* Boston: Casablanca Press, 1993.

Godek, Gregory J.P. *Romance 101.* Boston: Casablanca Press, 1993.

Hayden, Naura. *How to Satisfy a Woman Every Time...and Have Her Beg For More.* New York: Bibliophile Publishing, 1983.

Janus, Samual S., Ph.D., and Janus, Cynthia L., M.D. *The Janus Report on Sexual Behavior.* Reprinted. New York: John Wiley & Sons, 1994.

Klassen, Albert D., Williams, Colin J., and Levitt, Eugene E. *Sex and Morality in the U.S.* Middletown, Connecticut: Weslyan University Press, 1989.

Linfield, Jordan L., and Krvisky, Joseph. *Words of Love.* New York: Random House, 1997.

Kreidman, Ellen. *Light Her Fire: How to Ignite Passion and Excitement in the Women You Love.* New York: Villiard Books, 1991.

Masters, William Howell. *Human Sexual Response.* Boston: Little, 1966.

Michael, Robert T., Gagnon, John H., Laumann, Edward O., and Kolata, Gina. *Sex In America, A Definitive Survey.* New York: Warner Books, 1995.

Penney, Alexandra. *Great Sex.* New York: G.P. Putnam's Sons, 1985.

Reinisch, June M., Ph.D. *The Kinsey Institute New Report on Sex.* With Ruth Beasley. New York: St. Martins Press, 1990.

Westheimer, Dr. Ruth K. *Sex for Dummies.* California: IDG Books Worldwide, 1995.

Wolfe, Linda. *The Cosmo Report.* New York: Arbor House, 1981.

Zildbergh, Bernie, Ph.D. *The New Male Sexuality.* New York: Bantam Books, 1992.